WALCH PUBLISHING

D0999044

Daily Warm-Ups

GRAMMAR & USAGE

Level II

1   2   3   4   5   6   7   8   9   10

ISBN 0-8251-6055-3

Copyright © 2006

J. Weston Walch, Publisher

P.O. Box 658 • Portland, Maine 04104-0658

www.walch.com

Printed in the United States of America

Table of Contents

The *Daily Warm-Ups* series is a wonderful way to turn extra classroom minutes into valuable learning time. The 180 quick activities—one for each day of the school year—practice language arts skills. These daily activities may be used at the very beginning of class to get students into learning mode, near the end of class to make good educational use of that transitional time, in the middle of class to shift gears between lessons—or whenever else you have minutes that now go unused.

Daily Warm-Ups are easy-to-use reproducibles—simply photocopy the day's activity and distribute it. Or make a transparency of the activity and project it on the board. You may want to use the activities for extra-credit points or as a check on the language arts skills that are built and acquired over time.

However you choose to use them, *Daily Warm-Ups* are a convenient and useful supplement to your regular lesson plans. Make every minute of your class time count!

Concrete and Abstract Nouns

A **noun** is a word that names a person, place, thing, or idea.
Examples: musician, studio, guitar, hope

Nouns can be concrete or abstract. The examples listed above are all concrete except the noun *hope*.

Based on the examples listed above, explain the difference between a concrete and an abstract noun.

Think about some concrete and abstract nouns in your daily life. Make a list below.

Concrete   **Abstract**

Concrete or Abstract?

Remember that a **concrete noun** names a person, place, or thing that can be sensed with one of the five senses. An **abstract noun** names an idea or quality and cannot be sensed with one of the five senses.

For each of the following nouns, write **C** on the line if it is a concrete noun or **A** if it is an abstract noun.

____ 1. ocean

____ 2. aviary

____ 3. sorrow

____ 4. communication

____ 5. Earth

____ 6. beauty

____ 7. grandmother

____ 8. justice

____ 9. ability

____ 10. Miami

____ 11. bracelet

____ 12. belief

2

Common and Proper Nouns

A **common noun** names a person, place, or thing. A **proper noun** names a particular person, place, or thing.

> **Common nouns:** teacher, school, calendar
> **Proper nouns:** Mrs. Ramirez, Riverdale High School, September

Daily Warm-Ups: Grammar & Usage

Read the following sentences. Underline the common nouns once. Underline the proper nouns twice.

1. My grandmother came to the United States from Ireland before the Great Depression.

2. My brother usually drives us to school in his Toyota Camry.

3. Ryan works nights and weekends at Parker's Restaurant.

4. Aunt Hilda bought me an iPod for my birthday.

5. When I graduate from high school, I'm going to college at Boston University.

3

Parts of Speech

Making Proper Nouns

Remember that a **common noun** names a person, place, or thing.
A **proper noun** names a particular person, place, or thing.

Make each of the common nouns below into proper nouns. The first one has been done for you.

Daily Warm-Ups: Grammar & Usage

4

1. road *Baker Road* _____

2. river _____

3. store _____

4. teacher _____

5. aunt _____

6. park _____

7. month _____

8. school _____

9. car _____

10. holiday _____

Compound or Collective?

A **compound noun** is a noun that includes more than one word. Compound nouns may contain two or more words, hyphenated words, or two words that are combined as one.

Examples: dining room, babysitter, turtleneck

A **collective noun** names a group of people or things.

Examples: team, class, flock

Below is a list of compound and collective nouns. Create a two-column chart, labeling one column "Compound" and one column "Collective." Write the words in the appropriate columns.

first aid	crew	bystander
gang	league	orchestra
home run	paperback	greenhouse
post office	crowd	herd
group	tribe	motorcycle
washing machine	fish tank	software
sleeping bag	family	committee

5

Parts of Speech

Pronouns

A **pronoun** is a word that takes the place of one or more nouns. Pronouns are used to eliminate repetition in speaking and writing.

> **Example:** Rachel and Joey ran around the track until <u>they</u> got too tired.
>
> (*They* replaces the repetition of *Rachel and Joey*.)

The following sentences do not use pronouns. Rewrite the sentences using pronouns to avoid repetition.

1. Bianca and Erin went to the mall to shop for Bianca and Erin's prom dresses.

2. Bianca found the exact dress that Bianca was looking for.

3. Erin found a dress that Erin loved, but the dress wasn't Erin's size.

4. The salesperson helped Erin look for Erin's dress in another color.

Daily Warm-Ups: Grammar & Usage

6

Personal Pronouns

Complete the personal pronoun chart below.

First Person Singular Plural	
Second Person Singular Plural	
Third Person Singular Plural	

Daily Warm-Ups: Grammar & Usage

Pronouns and Antecedents

Recall that a pronoun is used to replace a noun to avoid unnecessary repetition. The word that the pronoun replaces is called its **antecedent**.

> **Example:** Veronica loves her new MP3 player. She uses it at the gym every day.
>
> (*Veronica* is the antecedent for *her* and *She*. *MP3 player* is the antecedent for *it*.)

As you can see in the example above, the antecedent can be in the same sentence as the pronoun, or it can be in the previous sentence.

Read the following sentences. Underline the pronouns, and circle their antecedents.

1. Mrs. Edwards always writes her comments at the end of the essays.

2. Jorge and Derek said they need a ride to school in the morning.

3. The gym was decorated more than it had been in previous years.

4. The mother woke up her children before they could wake up on their own.

5. Miranda failed her math test, so she will retake it next week.

Daily Warm-Ups: Grammar & Usage

8

Reflexive and Intensive Pronouns

Reflexive and intensive pronouns are formed by adding *-self* or *-selves* to personal pronouns.

> **Examples:** I usually make **myself** dinner if my parents work late. (reflexive)
>
> I **myself** do not enjoy biking. (intensive)

Read the following sentences. Underline each reflexive and intensive pronoun. Then decide if each one is reflexive (**R**) or intensive (**I**). Write the correct letter on the line before each sentence.

____ 1. The girl I babysit for finally learned to tie her shoes herself.

____ 2. You yourself can come to the benefit dance tomorrow night.

____ 3. Andrei bought himself new soccer cleats.

____ 4. The officer herself wrestled the criminal to the ground.

____ 5. I couldn't find myself in our class picture.

9

Indefinite Pronouns

Indefinite pronouns refer to unnamed people or things. They do not usually have definite antecedents.

> **Examples: Everyone** I invited is coming to the party.
>
> Have you seen **anybody** from class?

List as many indefinite pronouns as you can below. Then use three of them in sentences of your own.

Daily Warm-Ups: Grammar & Usage

10

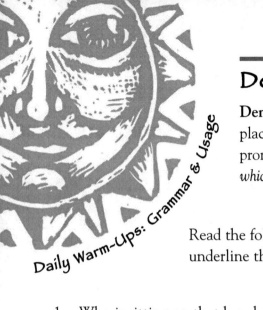

Demonstrative or Interrogative?

Demonstrative pronouns are used to point out specific people, places, or things. *This, that, these,* and *those* are all demonstrative pronouns. **Interrogative pronouns** are used to ask questions. *What, which, who, whom,* and *whose* are all interrogative pronouns.

Read the following sentences. Circle the demonstrative pronouns, and underline the interrogative pronouns.

1. Who is sitting on that bench?

2. Whose book is this?

3. Will you please pick up these papers?

4. Which one of you broke that lamp?

5. We bought those lamps on our trip to Europe.

6. What can I get for you?

Daily Warm-Ups: Grammar & Usage

11

Reviewing Pronouns

Remember that there are several different types of pronouns: personal, reflexive, intensive, indefinite, demonstrative, and interrogative.

Read each of the pronouns below. Write the type of each pronoun on the line provided.

Daily Warm-Ups: Grammar & Usage

12

1. himself _____

2. which _____

3. everyone _____

4. these _____

5. mine _____

6. someone _____

7. them _____

8. that _____

9. what _____

10. another _____

11. yours _____

12. myself _____

Take Action

An **action verb** tells what the subject of the sentence is doing.

Example: The baby **crawled** across the room to her mother.

Read each of the following sentences. Underline the action verbs. There may be more than one action verb in each sentence.

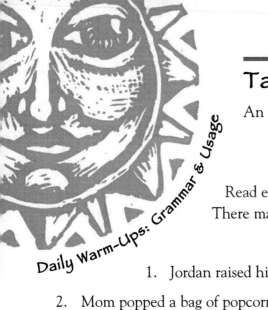

Daily Warm-Ups: Grammar & Usage

1. Jordan raised his hand and asked for help.

2. Mom popped a bag of popcorn in the microwave.

3. Josh flew on an airplane to Minneapolis.

4. Yukiko applied to six different colleges across the country.

5. The class rode the bus to the museum for a field trip.

6. Hector ate his dinner and then watched a movie.

13

Action or Being?

A **verb** is a word that expresses action or being. A sentence cannot exist without a verb.

> **Examples:** Taylor **ran** to the end of the street and back. (action)
>
> Now Taylor **is** exhausted. (being)

Daily Warm-Ups: Grammar & Usage

Read each of the following sentences. Decide whether each sentence contains a verb that expresses action or being. Write **A** on the line if it contains an action verb. Write **B** on the line if it contains a verb that expresses being.

14

___ 1. Kwame **took** his driver's test last week.

___ 2. He **made** a mistake parallel parking.

___ 3. Kwame **was** upset that he didn't pass his test.

___ 4. He **plans** on taking his test again next month.

___ 5. He **is** excited to try one more time.

Transitive and Intransitive Verbs

A **transitive verb** is a verb that has an object. An **intransitive verb** does not have an object. To find out if a verb has an object, ask the question *what?* or *whom?* after reading the verb.

Examples: I **walked** my dog around the block. (*Dog* is the object, so the verb is transitive.)

I **walked** around the block. (*Walked what? Walked whom?* There is no object, so the verb is intransitive.)

Decide if the verb is transitive (**T**) or intransitive (**I**). Write the correct letter on the line.

____ 1. Holly **rocked** her baby to sleep.

____ 2. Omar **ran** down the football field.

____ 3. He **scored** a touchdown just in time.

____ 4. Lindsay **raised** her hand to ask a question.

____ 5. John **drove** to the store to buy milk.

____ 6. Juanita **swam** across the lake and back.

15

Verb Phrases

A **verb phrase** is a group of words that contains a main verb and one or more helping verbs.

> **Example:** We **are going** to the supermarket on the way home. (*Going* is the main verb, and *are* is the helping verb.)

Helping verbs are often helpful to memorize. List as many helping verbs as you can below. Try to think of at least twenty.

16

More Verb Phrases

Remember that a **verb phrase** is a group of words that contains a main verb and one or more helping verbs.

Read the following sentences. Underline the verb phrases.

1. I will be finished in an hour.

2. You should write a letter to the editor.

3. We are giving you a ride to practice, right?

4. Jennifer is going to visit her grandparents for the holidays.

5. We might take a vacation next year.

6. You have been running for over an hour!

7. I was rushing to my appointment this morning.

8. They were looking for a place to stay.

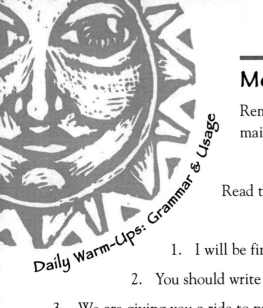

17

Daily Warm-Ups: Grammar & Usage

Linking Verbs

A **linking verb** is a verb or verb phrase that links the subject with another word in the sentence. The other word in the sentence names or describes the subject.

> **Examples:** Cecile **was** a freshman last year. (*Was* links *freshman* and *Cecile*.)
>
> You **must have been** proud of your students. (*Must have been* links *proud* and *you*.)

Linking verbs can be tricky. Remember that verbs are only linking verbs if they link the subject with another word that renames or describes the subject.

Read the following sentences. Write **Y** on the line if a sentence contains a linking verb and **N** on the line if it does not.

___ 1. This trip has been long and tiring.

___ 2. She was at the game until it ended.

___ 3. You are late again.

___ 4. I am tired of your excuses.

___ 5. You should have been here four hours ago!

Daily Warm-Ups: Grammar & Usage

Using Linking Verbs

Recall that a **linking verb** links the subject with another word in the sentence. The other word in the sentence names or describes the subject.

Write a paragraph about the outdoors using the following linking verbs:

was   have been   might be   seem   become

When you have finished writing your paragraph, circle the verb or verb phrase in each sentence. Then underline the two words or phrases that the verb links.

19

More Linking Verbs

The following verbs may also be used as linking verbs:

appear	feel	look	seem	sound	taste
become	grow	remain	smell	stay	turn

Use six of the linking verbs from the box above in sentences of your own.
Circle the words that rename or describe the subjects.

20

Verb Review

Remember that verbs can take many forms—action (**A**), transitive (**T**), intransitive (**I**), linking (**L**), helping (**H**). Keeping all of these forms in mind, underline the verbs in an essay or paper you have written recently. Label each verb or verb phrase with the correct letters listed above.

Adjectives

An **adjective** is a word that describes a noun or a pronoun. Most adjectives come before the nouns or pronouns they modify. Others come after the nouns or pronouns. Some come after linking verbs.

Examples: The **soft, cuddly** puppy fell asleep in my lap.
(before a noun)
The puppy, **soft** and **cuddly,** fell asleep in my lap.
(after a noun)
The puppy is **soft** and **cuddly.** (after a linking verb)

Read the following sentences. All the adjectives come before the noun. Rewrite each sentence so the adjectives come after the noun or after a linking verb.

1. The tall green grass needs to be mowed.

   _____

2. The heavy rain washed away all the pollen.

   _____

3. The child was afraid of the big, scary grizzly bear.

   _____

22

More Adjectives

Recall that adjectives are words that describe nouns and pronouns. Adjectives answer questions such as *What kind? Which one(s)? How many?* and *How much?*

Below is a list of several nouns. Write an adjective on the line before each noun. Use the questions above to help you think of adjectives.

1. _____ textbooks

2. _____ kitten

3. _____ bedroom

4. _____ desk

5. _____ car

6. _____ students

7. _____ picture

8. _____ women

9. _____ essay

10. _____ lamp

Proper and Compound Adjectives

A **proper adjective** begins with a capital letter and comes from a proper noun.

>   **Examples: French** bread, **Shakespearean** sonnet

A **compound adjective** contains more than one word. The words may be combined into one word, or they may be joined by a hyphen.

>   **Examples: brand-new** car, **ten-minute** presentation

Daily Warm-Ups: Grammar & Usage

Read the following sentences. Circle the proper adjectives, and underline the compound adjectives.

24

1. The well-dressed woman ducked into the French bistro.

2. My father gave me a fifteen-minute lecture about buying American cars.

3. The child was afraid of the three-headed monster in the movie.

4. For dessert we're having Boston cream pie.

5. The fair-skinned woman wore a long dress and high-heeled boots.

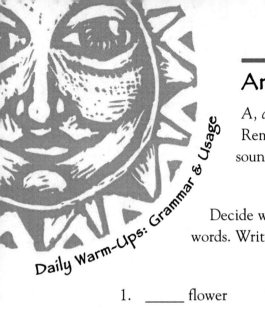

Articles

A, *an*, and *the* make up a group of adjectives called **articles.** Remember that *a* comes before words that begin with consonant sounds, and *an* comes before words that begin with vowel sounds.

Decide which article (*a* or *an*) should come before each of the following words. Write the correct article on the line.

1. _____ flower

2. _____ orange

3. _____ hour

4. _____ beverage

5. _____ performance

6. _____ igloo

7. _____ watch

8. _____ chain

9. _____ honor

10. _____ scientist

11. _____ adjective

12. _____ pineapple

Daily Warm-Ups: Grammar & Usage

25

Even More Adjectives

Read the following sentences. Underline all the adjectives, including articles.

1. My favorite contestant is the tall girl in the black dress.

2. We took a long, exhausting walk around the city.

3. The hurricane caused excessive damage to our home.

4. I received a gorgeous bouquet of flowers today.

5. My parents gave me a stunning gold bracelet for graduation.

6. The narrow street made it difficult to walk with traffic.

7. We had two delicious appetizers at the Italian restaurant.

8. The little girl wore a pink helmet to match her new bicycle.

26

Comparatives and Superlatives

Adjectives can be used to compare two or more things. The **comparative** compares two things and adds *-er* to the adjective. The comparative may also be formed by placing the word *more* in front of the adjective.

Examples: faster, more delicious

The **superlative** compares more than two things and adds *-est* to the adjective. Superlatives may also be formed by placing the word *most* in front of the adjective.

Examples: fastest, most delicious

Write five sentences about one of your favorite activities that contain comparatives and superlatives.

27

© 2006 Walch Publishing

Adverbs

An **adverb** is a word that modifies a verb, an adjective, or another adverb. Adverbs tell *how, when, where, how much,* and *why.* Many adverbs end with the letters *-ly.*

Examples: near, always, very, lovely

Read the words below. Check the words that are adverbs.

_____ 1. great

_____ 2. well

_____ 3. too

_____ 4. for

_____ 5. yesterday

_____ 6. carefully

_____ 7. bright

_____ 8. often

_____ 9. almost

_____ 10. nor

_____ 11. fast

_____ 12. windy

_____ 13. also

_____ 14. almost

_____ 15. unexpectedly

More Adverbs

Remember that an **adverb** is a word that modifies a verb, an adjective, or another adverb. Many adverbs end in *-ly*.

Change the following words into adverbs. Write the adverb on the line.

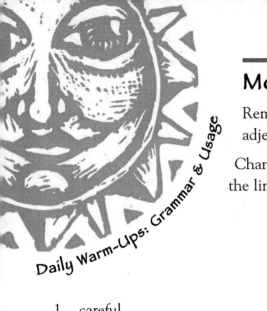

1. careful _____

2. basic _____

3. easy _____

4. comfortable _____

5. rare _____

6. happy _____

7. drastic _____

8. quick _____

9. equal _____

10. variable _____

11. bare _____

12. terrible _____

29

Adverbs in Action

Remember that an **adverb** is a word that modifies a verb, an adjective, or another adverb. Adverbs tell *how, when, where, how much*, and *why*. Many adverbs end with the letters *-ly*.

Underline the adverbs in the following sentences.

1. You're finished already? You completed the test too quickly.

2. The children quietly watched the movie and then went outside.

3. Sometimes I walk to school, but usually I take the bus.

4. Don't ever speak to me like that again!

5. Yesterday we took a field trip, and today we'll write a paper about it.

6. The students eagerly gathered near the gym.

7. I think I'll write more in my journal later.

8. You did rather well on your exam.

30

Writing with Adverbs

Remember that an **adverb** is a word that modifies a verb, an adjective, or another adverb. Adverbs tell *how, when, where, how much,* and *why.* Many adverbs end with the letters *-ly.*

Use the following adverbs in sentences of your own. Underline any additional adverbs in your sentences.

Daily Warm-Ups: Grammar & Usage

1. brightly, so

2. too, well

3. extremely, still

4. hard, today

5. sometimes, never

31

Adjectives and Adverbs

Remember that an adjective modifies a noun or a pronoun, and an adverb modifies a verb, an adjective, or another adverb.

Read each of the following sentences. Underline the adjectives and circle the adverbs.

Daily Warm-Ups: Grammar & Usage

32

1. We awoke to a blanket of fluffy white snow on the ground.

2. We patiently waited to see if we had a snow day.

3. When we got the news, I breathed a sigh of relief. I had an extra day to finish my ten-minute presentation.

4. I eagerly crawled back into my warm, cozy bed.

5. Fortunately, I could sleep for another three hours. I had stayed awake much too late the previous night.

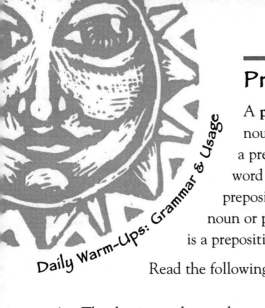

Prepositions

A **preposition** is a word that shows the relationship between a noun or pronoun and another word in the sentence. In order to be a preposition, the word must have an object. To determine if a word is a preposition, insert the word *what* or *whom* after the preposition. This will tell you if the preposition has an object. If a noun or pronoun answers the question of *what* or *whom*, then the word is a preposition.

Daily Warm-Ups: Grammar & Usage

Read the following sentences. Underline each preposition.

1. The dog jumped onto the couch.

2. I'm going to the movies with Emily tonight.

3. Please don't wait until Sunday to start your paper.

4. There will be no talking during the presentations.

5. Will you sit beside me at the assembly?

6. We went inside when it started raining.

33

Listing Prepositions

A **preposition** is a word that shows the relationship between a noun or a pronoun and another word in the sentence.

> **Example:** The skier came out **of** the gate and raced **down** the hill.

List as many prepositions as you can in the space below. You should be able to think of at least twenty.

34

Daily Warm-Ups: Grammar & Usage

Conjunctions

A **conjunction** is a word that joins other words or groups of words.
A **coordinating conjunction** is made up of one connecting word.
A **correlative conjunction** is made up of two connecting words.

Examples: and, but, or (coordinating)

either/or, neither/nor (correlative)

Underline the conjunctions in the following sentences.

1. Bring either your sneakers or your boots.

2. Whether we go to the fair or we stay home will depend on the weather.

3. I want to finish my homework, but I'd rather go to the mall.

4. Please run and get your book out of your locker.

5. I forgot not only my uniform but also my glove for the game today.

6. First we will review the material, and then we will have the quiz.

35

Combining with Conjunctions

Remember that a **conjunction** is a word that joins other words or groups of words. Use conjunctions to combine each of the following pairs of sentences into one. Try to vary the conjunctions that you use.

1. I remembered my book. I forgot my homework.

   _____

2. I got home from school early. I watched television for an hour.

   _____

3. I want to visit the art museum. I want to visit the museum of natural history.

   _____

4. I fell skiing down the mountain. I broke my wrist.

   _____

5. I got eleven hours of sleep last night. I still feel tired.

   _____

36

© 2006 Walch Publishing

Interjections

An **interjection** is a word or group of words that shows feeling. An interjection is separated from the rest of the sentence by a comma or an exclamation point.

Examples: Well, I have to start my homework.

Wow! You finished your homework already?

Write a sentence with an interjection to express each of the feelings listed below.

1. excitement _____

2. disappointment _____

3. fear _____

4. surprise _____

5. disbelief _____

37

© 2006 Walch Publishing

Parts of Speech

Review 1

Write two examples for each part of speech listed below.

Noun

_____

_____

Pronoun

_____

_____

Verb

_____

_____

Adjective

_____

_____

Adverb

_____

_____

Preposition

_____

_____

Conjunction

_____

_____

Interjection

_____

_____

38

Review II

Define and describe each of the eight parts of speech listed below.

1. noun _____

2. pronoun _____

3. verb _____

4. adjective _____

5. adverb _____

6. preposition _____

7. conjunction _____

8. interjection _____

Daily Warm-Ups: Grammar & Usage

39

Review III

Take a paragraph you have written recently and label each word with the correct part of speech. Use the following abbreviations to label the words:

noun (n.)	adverb (adv.)
pronoun (pn.)	preposition (prep.)
verb (v.)	conjunction (c.)
adjective (adj.)	interjection (int.)

Daily Warm-Ups: Grammar & Usage

40

Daily Warm-Ups: Grammar & Usage

What Is a Sentence?

A **sentence** is a group of words that expresses a complete thought. A sentence contains a subject (noun) and a predicate (verb). If a group of words does not contain a subject and a predicate, it is not a sentence; it is a fragment.

Examples: Ramon ran to the store. (sentence)

Ran to the store. (fragment)

Read the following groups of words. Write **S** on the line if it is a sentence. Write **F** on the line if it is a fragment.

___ 1. Kim took her driver's test yesterday.

___ 2. She failed.

___ 3. Will take it again next month.

___ 4. She is extremely disappointed.

___ 5. Practice makes perfect.

___ 6. Making left-hand turns.

41

Fragments to Sentences

Remember that a sentence contains a subject and a predicate. If it does not, then it is a fragment.

Turn the following fragments into sentences. Write the sentence on the line. Make sure it includes a subject and a predicate.

1. the chicken in your salad _____

_____

2. from one place to another _____

_____

42

3. the soccer ball in the goal _____

_____

4. with my mother _____

_____

5. to pick up some milk _____

_____

Types of Sentences

There are four types of sentences: declarative, imperative, interrogative, and exclamatory.

Declarative: makes a statement

Imperative: gives a command/direction, or makes a request

Interrogative: asks a question

Exclamatory: expresses strong feeling or emotion

Read the following sentences. Write the type of sentence on the line.

1. Where are you going? _____

2. Please don't stay out too late. _____

3. You look absolutely stunning in that dress! _____

4. I want to go camping this summer. _____

5. Will you help me with this assignment? _____

6. Take your feet off the table. _____

7. We are taking a vacation to Hawaii next year. _____

8. Ouch! That bee sting hurts! _____

43

Subjects and Predicates

Remember that a sentence is a group of words that contains a subject and a predicate. A subject is a noun or pronoun, and a predicate is a verb.

>**Example:** Brooke tiptoed down the hallway.
>
>(*Brooke* is the subject, and *tiptoed* is the predicate.)

Read the following sentences. After each sentence, write the subject on the first line and the predicate on the second line.

Daily Warm-Ups: Grammar & Usage

1. The puppy played with the older dog all day.

   _____   _____

2. Henry bought a new MP3 player with his birthday money.

   _____   _____

3. Kaylee locked her keys in her car.

   _____   _____

4. Kyle took the bus to the mall after school.

   _____   _____

44

Complete and Simple Subjects

A **complete subject** is a group of words that names what a sentence is about.

> **Example: The tall boy out in left field** made a great diving catch.

A **simple subject** is the main word (noun or pronoun) in the complete subject.

> **Example:** The tall **boy** out in left field made a great diving catch.

Read the following sentences. Underline the complete subjects, and circle the simple subjects.

1. A slice of apple pie is my ideal dessert.

2. The little black dog chased our car down the street.

3. The lady across the street baked us cookies when we moved in.

4. My sister Tiana knows how to make jewelry.

5. Anthony was late to class today.

Daily Warm-Ups: Grammar & Usage

45

Complete and Simple Predicates

A **complete predicate** is a group of words that tells something about the subject.

> **Example:** Juan **runs on the treadmill at the gym.**

A **simple predicate** is the main word or phrase in the complete predicate.

> **Example:** Juan **runs** on the treadmill at the gym.

Read the following sentences. Underline the complete predicates, and circle the simple predicates.

1. The little black dog chased our car down the street.

2. The lady across the street baked us cookies when we moved in.

3. My sister Tiana knows how to make jewelry.

4. That teacher always gives tests on Mondays.

Now write two sentences of your own that contain complete and simple predicates.

46

Daily Warm-Ups: Grammar & Usage

Compound Subjects

A **compound subject** contains two or more subjects, uses the same verb, and is joined by a conjunction such as *and* or *or*.

Examples: <u>Joaquin</u>, <u>Brandon</u>, **and** <u>Michael</u> played basketball after school.

<u>Mom</u> **or** <u>Dad</u> will pick you up after practice today.

Daily Warm-Ups: Grammar & Usage

Complete the following sentences with compound subjects.

1. _____ are my favorite foods.

2. _____ helped make dinner and set the table.

3. _____ decorated for the party.

4. _____ are going to the dance together.

5. _____ were absent from class today.

47

Compound Verbs

A **compound verb** contains two or more verbs, uses the same subject, and is joined by a conjunction such as *and* or *or*.

> **Examples:** Barron <u>washed</u> **and** <u>dried</u> the dishes after dinner.
> Kenya <u>pitched</u> a tent **and** <u>built</u> a fire.

Read the following sentences. Write **Y** on the line if the sentence contains a compound verb, and write **N** if it does not.

_____ 1. Jenna and I will pick you up and take you to the play.

_____ 2. Kevin is taking a nap, and Montell is reading a book.

_____ 3. You should either do your homework or fill out your applications.

_____ 4. The robber put the car in drive and sped away.

_____ 5. Grandma told us to rake and bag the leaves.

_____ 6. Aysha and Grace visited many colleges in the Northeast.

48

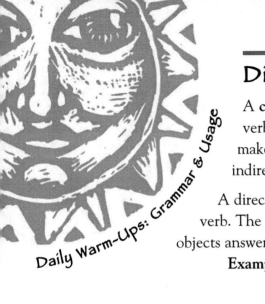

Direct Objects

A **complement** is part of a sentence that follows the subject and verb. Complements are sometimes necessary for the sentence to make sense. There are four types of complements: direct objects, indirect objects, predicate nominatives, and predicate adjectives.

A direct object is a noun or pronoun that receives the action of the verb. The verb used with a direct object is always an action verb. Direct objects answer the question What? or Whom?

Example: Jason hit a **grand slam.**

Complete each of the following sentences with a direct object.

1. Nadia watched _____

2. The doctor examined _____

3. Mr. Gallagher teaches _____

4. Cedric caught _____.

5. Lily takes _____

49

Indirect Objects

An indirect object is part of a sentence that follows an action verb. It answers one of the following questions: *To whom? For whom? To what? For what?* The indirect object always comes between the verb and the direct object.

>**Example:** Rashid gave his **teacher** a gift.

Underline the direct object in each of the following sentences.

1. Mom brought me my lunch.

2. I made you a turkey sandwich.

3. Mrs. Robinson gave her class homework for the weekend.

4. Madison told me to say hello to you.

5. I'll get you a drink when I'm at the store.

6. Please save Ella a piece of cake.

Direct or Indirect?

Remember that a **direct object** is a noun or pronoun that receives the action of the verb. An **indirect object** is a noun that tells to whom or for whom something is done. The indirect object always comes between the verb and the direct object.

Read the following sentences. Label the parts of each sentence. Use **V** for verb, **D** for direct object, and **I** for indirect object.

1. Lila sent Mr. Hernandez an e-mail.

2. We gave my grandmother a gift certificate for Mother's Day.

3. The dentist mailed my parents a bill for my cleaning.

4. The little girl made her father a card for his birthday.

5. Mrs. Adams read her kindergartners a story before their snack.

6. The pitcher threw the batter a 95-mile-an-hour fastball.

51

Daily Warm-Ups: Grammar & Usage

Predicate Nominatives

Complements that follow linking verbs are called **subject complements.** A **predicate nominative** is a noun or pronoun that completes the linking verb. It identifies, explains, or renames the subject of the sentence.

> **Example:** Mrs. O'Connor is my favorite **teacher.**

Read the following sentences. Circle the predicate nominative. Then draw an arrow from the predicate nominative to the subject.

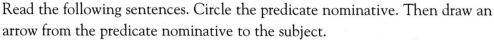

1. Emily is a fabulous dancer.

2. Dogs are the best pets.

3. Mr. Lopez became an instructor after only one year.

4. Sanjay is the best player on the team.

5. John has been an asset to the committee.

Daily Warm-Ups: Grammar & Usage

Compound Predicate Nominatives

Remember that a **predicate nominative** is a noun or pronoun that completes the linking verb. It identifies, explains, or renames the subject of the sentence. A **compound predicate nominative** contains two or more predicate nominatives that follow the same linking verb.

> **Example:** Our pets' names are **Rocco, Phoebe,** and **Jester.**

Read the following sentences. Write **Y** on the line if it contains a compound predicate nominative. Write **N** if it does not.

___ 1. Raquel and Rosa are not twins.

___ 2. My favorite foods are pizza, scrambled eggs, and chicken fingers.

___ 3. The students who scored highest on the test were Jack and Marcia.

___ 4. The next class president will be either Juan or Greg.

___ 5. The next class president should be Ana.

___ 6. Mrs. Nguyen is the best teacher in the school.

53

Making Predicate Nominatives

Remember that a **predicate nominative** is a noun or pronoun that completes the linking verb. It identifies, explains, or renames the subject of the sentence. Predicate nominatives can be compound.

Use the following words to write sentences that contain predicate nominatives. The words listed below should be part of the predicate nominative.

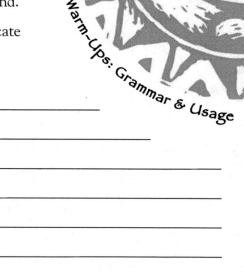

1. Dan, Matt, and David _____

   _____

2. the best snack _____

   _____

3. soccer, basketball, and baseball _____

   _____

4. our substitute teacher today _____

   _____

54

Predicate Adjectives

Remember that complements that follow linking verbs are called **subject complements.** A **predicate adjective** is an adjective that follows a linking verb and describes the subject.

Example: The dog was afraid of its own shadow.

Afraid describes *the dog.*

Daily Warm-Ups: Grammar & Usage

Read the following sentences. Circle the predicate adjective in each sentence. Then draw an arrow from the predicate adjective to the subject.

1. The new teacher was very shy on her first day of school.

2. Those flowers are absolutely beautiful!

3. It will be too hot to play the softball game today.

4. That dog is old and tired.

5. My biology teacher is so smart.

55

Predicate Adjectives vs. Regular Adjectives

Be sure not to confuse predicate adjectives with regular adjectives. Remember that predicate adjectives follow linking verbs and describe the subject.

> **Examples:** Dogs make **great** pets. (regular adjective)
> Dogs are **great.** (predicate adjective)

Read the following sentences. Write **PA** on the line if the sentence contains a predicate adjective. Write **RA** on the line if it contains a regular adjective.

___ 1.   Mr. Davis is a wonderful teacher.

___ 2.   Vinnie is always cordial to people he meets.

___ 3.   This test will be easy.

___ 4.   This test will be an easy one.

___ 5.   Florida is nice this time of year.

___ 6.   Florida is a nice place to visit.

Sentences

Reviewing Subject Complements

Remember that predicate nominatives and predicate adjectives are types of subject complements. These are complements that follow linking verbs.

Read the following sentences. Decide if the words in bold are predicate nominatives (**PN**) or predicate adjectives (**PA**). Write the appropriate letters on the line before each statement.

_____ 1.   Sammy was the best **dog.**

_____ 2.   He was so **playful** and **fun.**

_____ 3.   Tomorrow will be **rainy.**

_____ 4.   Luisa is **excited** to see her son.

_____ 5.   Janice is a **student** at the local university.

_____ 6.   Jonathan will become a **doctor** someday.

_____ 7.   You are an **inspiration** to all of us.

_____ 8.   Clarence is **good** at crossword puzzles.

57

Reviewing Sentences I

Write a definition for each of the sentence parts below. If you
have trouble defining each part, write an example.

1. compound subject _____

   _____

2. compound verb _____

   _____

3. direct object _____

   _____

4. indirect object _____

   _____

5. predicate nominative _____

   _____

6. predicate adjective _____

   _____

58

Reviewing Sentences II

Write a sentence that contains each of the following parts.

1. compound subject _____

   _____

2. compound verb _____

   _____

3. direct object _____

   _____

4. indirect object _____

   _____

5. predicate nominative _____

   _____

6. predicate adjective _____

   _____

Daily Warm-Ups: Grammar & Usage

59

Reviewing Sentences III

Write a paragraph about what you did last night. Label the parts of each sentence. Use the abbreviations below as labels.

complete subject (CS)

simple subject (SS)

complete predicate (CP)

simple predicate (SP)

compound subject (CDS)

compound verb (CV)

direct object (DO)

indirect object (IO)

predicate nominative (PN)

predicate adjective (PA)

60

Prepositional Phrases

A **phrase** is a group of words that functions as a single part of speech. A **prepositional phrase** begins with a preposition and must always end with an object. The object is always a noun or a pronoun.

Example: Take your feet **off the desk** and put them **on the floor.**

Rewrite the following sentences, adding a prepositional phrase to each one.

1. We took a class field trip to the museum.

2. We saw several interesting exhibits.

3. Then we ate lunch at the museum café.

4. The ride home was long and tiresome.

5. Overall, we had a great day.

61

Adjective Phrases

There are two types of prepositional phrases: adjective phrases and adverb phrases. **Adjective phrases** are used to modify nouns or pronouns. Adjective phrases answer the following questions: *Which ones?* and *What kind?* An adjective phrase immediately follows the noun or pronoun it modifies.

> **Example:** I met the woman **in the red dress** last week.

Read the following sentences. Underline the adjective phrases and circle the nouns or pronouns they modify.

62

1. The little girl on the bus waved to her mother.

2. The students in the auditorium waited patiently for the guest speaker.

3. The homework for that class is always so difficult.

4. The bedroom was painted an ugly shade of pink.

5. The baby across the hall is always crying.

Adverb Phrases

Adverb phrases are prepositional phrases used to modify verbs, adjectives, or adverbs. Adverb phrases tell *how, when, where, how much,* and *why.*

> **Examples:** Will you please take me **to school**? (where)
> **Because you were late,** you missed the lesson. (why)

Read the following sentences. Underline the adverb phrases and circle the verbs, adjectives, or adverbs they modify.

1. Are you angry with me?

2. I crossed the finish line with great satisfaction.

3. We slept during our flight.

4. Because of our hunger, we ordered an appetizer.

5. I can pass the test with your help.

63

More Adverb Phrases

Remember that an adverb phrase is a prepositional phrase used to
modify verbs, adjectives, or adverbs. Adverb phrases tell *how,
when, where, how much,* and *why.*

Read the following sentences, paying close attention to the adverb
phrases in bold. Decide what the adverb phrase is doing in the sentence.
On the line before each sentence, write *how, when, where, how much,* or *why.*

_____ 1. Are you going **to the mall** later?

_____ 2. I crossed the finish line **with great satisfaction.**

_____ 3. We slept **during our flight.**

_____ 4. **Because of our hunger,** we ordered an appetizer.

_____ 5. I can pass the test **with your help.**

_____ 6. Mrs. Leland lives **down the street.**

Adjective Phrase or Adverb Phrase?

Remember that an **adjective phrase** is a prepositional phrase used to modify nouns or pronouns. Adjective phrases answer the following questions: *Which ones?* and *What kind?* An **adverb phrase** is a prepositional phrase used to modify verbs, adjectives, or adverbs. Adverb phrases tell *how, when, where, how much,* and *why.*

Read each of the following sentences and decide if it contains an adjective phrase (**ADJ**) or an adverb phrase (**ADV**). Write the appropriate abbreviation on the line before each sentence.

_____ 1.   The woman by the dock will be your instructor.

_____ 2.   The little girl talked during the whole movie.

_____ 3.   Will you please pick me up at 3:30?

_____ 4.   All of the tickets are sold out.

_____ 5.   You will get a detention because of your tardiness.

_____ 6.   The man with Joanna is her boyfriend.

Appositives and Appositive Phrases

An **appositive** is a noun or pronoun that identifies or explains another noun or pronoun in the sentence. An **appositive phrase** is a group of words that identifies or renames the noun or pronoun that it follows.

> **Examples:** My older sister, **Sarah,** works at the mall after school. (appositive)
>
> Sarah, **my older sister,** works at the mall after school. (appositive phrase)

Read the following sentences. Circle the appositives, and underline the appositive phrases.

1. My brother, Tyrone, is going to college in the fall.

2. Have you read *The Bell Jar*, a book by Sylvia Plath?

3. Boston, the capital city of Massachusetts, is my favorite place to visit.

4. The guitar, my favorite instrument, is easy to play.

5. My physics teacher, Mr. Manchester, is out sick today.

66

Appositives and Commas

Appositives and appositive phrases may or may not need to be set off by commas. If an appositive contains information that is necessary to understand the meaning of the sentence, no commas are needed.

> **Example:** Anne's friend **Michael** helped her with the assignment.
>
> (Anne has more than one friend, so the information is necessary.)

If an appositive contains information that is unnecessary to understand the meaning of the sentence, commas should separate the appositive from the rest of the sentence.

> **Example:** Sasha's mother, **Chantal,** just had an operation.
>
> (Sasha only has one mother, so the information is unnecessary.)

Write five sentences of your own that contain appositives. Use commas when appropriate.

67

© 2006 Walch Publishing

Adding Appositives

Remember that an **appositive** is a noun or pronoun that identifies or explains another noun or pronoun in the sentence. An **appositive phrase** is a group of words that identifies or renames the noun or pronoun that it follows.

Rewrite each of the following sentences with an appositive or an appositive phrase. Be sure to use commas properly.

1. When I was much younger, my family went to Disney World on vacation.

2. Kerri plans to attend New York University in the fall.

68

3. My parents grew up in Washington state.

4. Derek Jeter has been an all-star shortstop for many years.

5. I have to e-mail my chemistry teacher to ask her about our assignment.

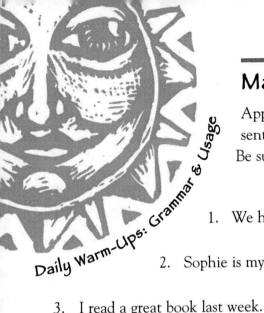

Making Appositives

Appositives and appositive phrases can be used to eliminate short sentences. Combine the following sentences by using appositives. Be sure to use commas properly.

1. We had brownie sundaes for dessert. They are my favorite.

2. Sophie is my cousin. She plays the violin well.

3. I read a great book last week. It was called *The Joy Luck Club*.

4. Have you seen Pedro? He is my parents' friend.

5. The Morins are moving next week. They are our neighbors.

6. Britney pulled a ligament in a race. She is a skier.

69

Participles

A **verbal** is a verb form used as another part of speech. A **verbal phrase** is a verbal with modifiers. There are three types of verbals: participles, gerunds, and infinitives.

A **participle** is a verb form that is used as an adjective. This means that it describes a noun or a pronoun. A participle answers the questions *Which one(s)?* and *What kind?*

> **Examples: broken** leg, **failing** students

Participles take two forms: present and past. Present participles end in *-ing,* and past participles usually end in *-ed.* Sometimes past participles have more irregular endings such as *-n, -t,* or *-en.*

Read the following sentences. Underline the participles.

1. I ate burnt toast for breakfast this morning.

2. The motorcycle came to a screeching stop.

3. The howling wolf scared the camping family.

4. His torn shirt was a result of the accident.

70

Participle Fill-in

Remember that participles take two forms: present and past.
Present participles end in *-ing*, and past participles usually end in
-ed. Sometimes past participles have more irregular endings such as
-n, *-t*, or *-en*.

Add a participle to each of the following nouns.

1. _____ rain

2. _____ students

3. _____ sun

4. _____ car

5. _____ road

6. _____ dog

7. _____ house

8. _____ blanket

9. _____ bird

10. _____ ocean

11. _____ food

12. _____ boat

71

© 2006 Walch Publishing

Participial Phrases

A **participial phrase** is a phrase that works as an adjective. The phrase contains a participle and its complement(s) and modifies the subject of the sentence.

> **Examples: Racing around the track,** the horse moved into first place.
>
> The party, **hosted by Jasmine,** was a great success.

Read the following sentences. Underline the participial phrases and circle the words they modify.

1. Driving to school, Raymond realized he forgot his homework.

2. Reviewing her notes, Jackie felt ready for the test.

3. The test, printed on both sides of the paper, took me two hours.

4. Tired from his long day, Kasim rested on the couch.

5. Mrs. Goodman, walking up and down the aisles, lectured us on plagiarism.

72

Commas in Participial Phrases

When a participial phrase comes at the beginning of a sentence, it is followed by a comma. When it comes in the middle of a sentence, it may or may not need a comma. If the information in the phrase is necessary for the sentence to make sense, no commas are needed.

Example: The child **swimming in the lake** is my younger brother.

If the information in the phrase is unnecessary for the sentence to make sense, then the phrase should be set off by commas.

Example: My brother, **swimming in the lake,** turns seven next month.

Read the following sentences. Underline the participial phrases and add any necessary commas.

1. Landing safely on the runway the plane neared the airport.

2. The children covered in mud ran through the kitchen.

3. The vegetables grown in my garden are organic.

4. The students talking during the movie had to stay after class.

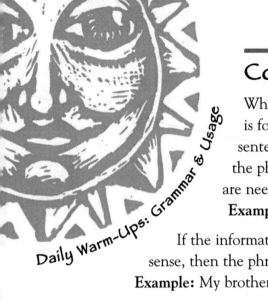

Daily Warm-Ups: Grammar & Usage

73

Gerunds

A **gerund** is a verb that is used as a noun. Gerunds are usually created by adding *-ing*.

Read the following sentences. Put a check mark next to those that contain a gerund.

____ 1. Mia was running down the soccer field.

____ 2. Talking on instant messenger and writing e-mails are my favorite things to do after school.

____ 3. Brian enjoys walking to work when it isn't raining.

____ 4. Dinah was caught cheating on the test.

____ 5. Malcolm's favorite activity is swimming.

74

Now write two sentences about yourself using gerunds.

Gerund Phrases

A **gerund phrase** is a phrase that contains a gerund and its complements to make up a noun.

> **Examples: Backpacking across Europe** is certainly a great idea.
>
> **Drawing portraits** is Anna's favorite thing to do.

Read the following sentences. Underline the gerund phrases.

1. Hiking up the mountain will be difficult for my mother because she has a bad back.

2. I was doing my homework for four hours last night.

3. I found my father outside raking the lawn.

4. Flying over the Grand Canyon was an amazing experience.

5. I think smoking cigarettes is disgusting.

6. Pushing this button will turn off the computer.

75

Writing Gerund Phrases

Remember that a **gerund phrase** is a phrase that contains a gerund and its complements to make up a noun.

> **Examples: Backpacking across Europe** is certainly a great idea.
>
> **Drawing portraits** is Anna's favorite thing to do.

Use the *-ing* words below to write sentences containing gerund phrases.

1. traveling

2. identifying

3. working

4. writing

5. camping

6. collecting

Daily Warm-Ups: Grammar & Usage

76

Confusing Participles and Gerunds

Participles that end in *-ing* can be easily confused with gerunds. Participles are used as adjectives, and gerunds are used as nouns.

Read the following sentences. Write **P** on the line if the sentence contains a participle, and write **G** on the line if the sentence contains a gerund.

___ 1. Talking during class is not allowed unless you are called on.

___ 2. The winding road was dangerous to drive.

___ 3. Aware of the approaching snowstorm, the students hoped school would be canceled.

___ 4. Terri enjoys kayaking during the summer.

___ 5. You spend too much time playing video games.

___ 6. The freezing rain made the roads very slick.

77

Infinitives

An **infinitive** is a verb form that usually begins with the word *to* and is used as a noun, an adjective, or an adverb. Infinitives are often confused with prepositional phrases because they both start with *to*.

> **Examples:** I love **to play** field hockey. (infinitive)
>
> You should come **to my next field hockey game.** (prepositional phrase)

Find a paper or essay that you have recently written. Label all the infinitives with an **I** and all the prepositional phrases with a **P.**

78

Infinitive Phrases

Remember that an **infinitive** is a verb form that usually begins with the word *to* and is used as a noun, an adjective, or an adverb. An **infinitive phrase** contains an infinitive and its modifiers.

Examples: I asked Mr. Aube **to explain the worksheet.**
We went **to see a play** for our class field trip.

Daily Warm-Ups: Grammar & Usage

Read the following sentences. Underline the infinitive phrases.

1. I asked you to speak clearly.

2. I would like to send flowers to the neighbors.

3. To pass the test requires several hours of studying.

4. I want to try surfing when we go to Hawaii.

5. To avoid getting in trouble, Claire lied about where she had been.

6. I have been known to change my mind.

79

Reviewing Verbals

Remember that verbals are verb forms that are used as another part of speech. These include participles, gerunds, and infinitives. Participles are used as adjectives; gerunds are used as nouns; and infinitives begin with *to* and are used as nouns, adjectives, or adverbs.

Read the following sentences and decide what type of verbal each sentence contains. Write **P** for participle, **G** for gerund, and **I** for infinitive.

____ 1. Skiing is my favorite winter sport.

____ 2. That team will be hard to beat.

____ 3. You can walk out on the frozen lake.

____ 4. The child was afraid of the barking dog.

____ 5. Riding my bike is something I don't do nearly enough.

____ 6. The birthday card, written in cursive, looked odd.

____ 7. That chicken has to be eaten before it spoils.

____ 8. Will you please try to help me?

80

Introduction to Clauses

A **clause** is a group of words that contains a subject and a verb. A clause is different from a phrase in that it contains a subject and a verb, and a phrase does not. Like phrases, clauses can be used as nouns, adjectives, and adverbs.

> **Examples:** I'll take a shower **after breakfast.** (phrase)
> I'll take a shower **after I eat breakfast.** (clause)
> (*I* is the subject of the clause, and *eat* is the verb.)

Read the following phrases and clauses. Write **P** on the line for each phrase and **C** for each clause.

____ 1. when you finish

____ 2. to the mall

____ 3. the librarian at school

____ 4. before Carrie went to sleep

____ 5. after school

____ 6. by the stairs

____ 7. as Rico drove by

____ 8. when I wake up

81

Daily Warm-Ups: Grammar & Usage

Independent Clauses

An **independent clause** can stand alone as a sentence because it expresses a complete thought. It is also known as the **main clause** of the sentence. If an independent clause stands alone, it is called a sentence. If it is paired with another clause, it is called a clause.

> **Examples:** Julio went to practice, and Kara went home. (clause)
>
> Julio went to practice. Kara went home. (sentence)

Combine the following sentences into independent clauses.

82

1. I am going to bed. You should, too.

_____

2. Grant's birthday is in April. Selim's is in May.

_____

3. I have Mr. Lopez for English. My sister has Mrs. Thomas.

_____

4. My favorite class is biology. Shannon's is geometry.

_____

Subordinate Clauses

A **subordinate clause** cannot stand alone as a sentence. It does not express a complete thought. Subordinate clauses are also called **dependent clauses** because they *depend* on another clause to form a complete sentence.

> **Example: After he ran,** Cameron took a shower. (*After he ran* does not express a complete thought.)

Rewrite the following sentences with subordinate clauses.

1. Lian got his license.

   _____

2. We rented a movie last night.

   _____

3. Lena got a letter from Clemson University.

   _____

4. Please set the table.

   _____

83

Daily Warm-Ups: Grammar & Usage

Independent or Subordinate?

Remember that a **clause** is a group of words that contains a subject and a verb. An **independent clause** is the main clause of a sentence. It expresses a complete thought and can stand alone as a sentence. A **subordinate clause** cannot stand alone. It needs to be paired with an independent clause to make a complete sentence.

Daily Warm-Ups: Grammar & Usage

Example: After he finished his homework, Theo ate dinner.

      (subordinate clause)   **(independent clause)**

Read each of the following clauses. Write **I** on the line if it is an independent clause and **S** on the line if it is a subordinate clause.

84

_____ 1.   because we were running late

_____ 2.   Devon brought his laptop to class

_____ 3.   after you get the directions

_____ 4.   he asked me to help him

_____ 5.   we watched television for most of the night

_____ 6.   when the airplane landed

Adverb Clauses

Subordinate clauses can be used as nouns, adjectives, and adverbs. An **adverb clause** is a clause that acts as a verb and modifies a verb, adjective, or adverb. It usually modifies a verb. An adverb clause answers *How? When? Where? Why? How much?* and *Under what condition?*

Example: Stay away from a dog **when it's growling.**

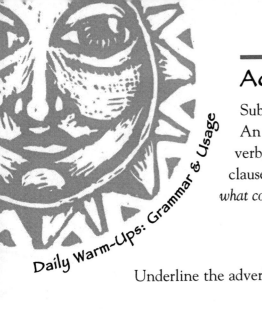

Underline the adverb clauses in the following sentences.

1. We will leave whenever your mother gets home.

2. We'll take the bus if it rains tomorrow.

3. I put my essay in my bag so I wouldn't forget it.

4. They got to the movie after it had started.

5. You grill the steak while I make the salad.

6. Take the cookies out of the oven before they burn.

85

© 2006 Walch Publishing

Modifying Adjectives and Adverbs

Most adverb clauses modify verbs, but some modify adjectives
and adverbs.

Examples: My sister is <u>older</u> **than I am.** (adjective)

You drove more <u>carefully</u> **than I did.** (adverb)

Write five sentences of your own containing adverb clauses that modify
adjectives and adverbs.

Daily Warm-Ups: Grammar & Usage

86

Subordinating Conjunctions

An adverb clause begins with a **subordinating conjunction.** Look at the list of subordinating conjunctions below.

after	before	until
although	if	when
as	since	whenever
as if	than	where
as though	though	wherever
because	unless	while

Use the list above to write five sentences that contain adverb clauses. Underline the subordinating conjunction, and circle the word that the clause modifies.

87

Daily Warm-Ups: Grammar & Usage

Adjective Clauses

An **adjective clause** is a type of subordinate clause that is used to modify a noun or a pronoun. The clause is used as an adjective. Adjective clauses answer *Which one(s)?* and *What kind?*

> **Example:** The person **who is at the door** is looking for Mom.

Underline the adjective clauses in the following sentences.

1. The book, which is downstairs on the coffee table, only took a few hours to read.

2. Andy is driving a car that has a headlight out.

3. The man who got in the car accident was rushed to the hospital.

4. This is the route that we take every day.

5. I am looking for the student who wrote this paper.

6. I like a teacher who takes a hands-on approach.

7. The shoes that I just bought are extremely uncomfortable.

8. The teacher who gave that assignment is Mr. McDonald.

88

Daily Warm-Ups: Grammar & Usage

More Adjective Clauses

Remember that an **adjective clause** is a type of subordinate clause that is used to modify a noun or a pronoun. Adjective clauses usually begin with relative pronouns. These include *who, whom, whose, which,* and *that*. Adjective clauses can also begin with *when* and *where*.

Read the following sentences. Underline the adjective clauses. Circle the relative pronouns.

1. Are those the shoes that you bought last week?

2. You got the shoes when we went shopping, right?

3. Here is where we stayed for the wedding.

4. The college that Isabel attends is in New York.

5. Everyone who passed the test will not have to take the final.

6. We ate pizza, which was left over from dinner, for lunch.

89

Combining Adjective Clauses

Adjective clauses can be used to create more interesting sentences. Use adjective clauses to combine the following sentences. Use the words in the box below to begin the clauses.

| who | whom | whose | which | that | when | where |

1. The waiter brought us our breakfast. His name escapes me.

_____

2. The store is in the mall. I bought my jeans there.

_____

3. My mother rented me a movie. It is about airplanes.

_____

4. The restaurant was shut down. The customers got food poisoning.

_____

5. My sister goes everywhere in her car. She bought it herself.

_____

90

© 2006 Walch Publishing

Adjective Clauses and Commas

Adjective clauses do not need to be set off by commas if the information in the clause is necessary for the sentence to make sense.

>**Example:** The person **who robbed the bank** is from a neighboring town.

Adjective clauses should be set off by commas if the clause contains information that is not necessary to make sense of the sentence.

>**Example:** The bank robber, **who is from a neighboring town,** got away with over $10,000.

Read the following sentences. Add commas where necessary.

1. Our neighbor who makes a great apple pie is Mrs. Kimball.

2. The woman who makes the apple pie is Mrs. Kimball.

3. That book which is the best book I have ever read is over there.

4. The place where she works is all the way on the other side of town.

5. The dog that bit me now has to wear a muzzle.

Daily Warm-Ups: Grammar & Usage

91

Noun Clauses

A **noun clause** is a subordinate clause that can be used as a noun or a pronoun. It can be a subject, predicate nominative, direct object, appositive, indirect object, or object of the preposition.

> **Example: Whatever you want to do** is okay with me.

Noun clauses can begin with the same words that begin adjective clauses. They may begin with any of the words in the box below.

Daily Warm-Ups: Grammar & Usage

how	what	where	who	whomever
if	whatever	whether	whoever	whose
that	when	which	whom	why

92

Underline the noun clauses in the following sentences.

1. How much I weigh is none of your business.

2. The award goes to whoever writes the best essay.

3. A quick dinner is what I can handle right now.

4. Do you know where diamonds are found?

5. Everyone wants to know how he did the trick.

Writing Noun Clauses

Remember that a **noun clause** is a subordinate clause that can be used as a noun or a pronoun.

Add a noun clause to complete each sentence below. Write the sentence on the line.

Daily Warm-Ups: Grammar & Usage

1. her struggle is _____

2. do you know _____

3. is an accomplishment _____

4. the money will go to _____

5. is a mystery to us _____

93

Subordinate Clause Review

Remember that an **adverb clause** is a clause that acts as a verb and modifies a verb, adjective, or adverb. An **adjective clause** is a clause that is used to modify a noun or a pronoun. A **noun clause** is a clause that can be used as a noun or a pronoun.

Decide what type of subordinate clause each of the following sentences contains. Write **ADV** for adverb clause, **ADJ** for adjective clause, and **N** for noun clause.

Daily Warm-Ups: Grammar & Usage

_____ 1.   The man who works behind the counter is my uncle.

_____ 2.   How you want to pay me back is up to you.

_____ 3.   You can go if you finish your homework in time.

_____ 4.   I was late because I overslept.

_____ 5.   The man who is at the door wants to see you.

_____ 6.   Did you know that we can stay an extra day?

_____ 7.   I have a lot of homework that I have to do tonight.

_____ 8.   We left as soon as the concert ended.

94

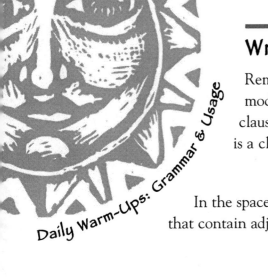

Daily Warm-Ups: Grammar & Usage

Writing Subordinate Clauses

Remember that an **adverb clause** is a clause that acts as a verb and modifies a verb, adjective, or adverb. An **adjective clause** is a clause that is used to modify a noun or a pronoun. A **noun clause** is a clause that can be used as a noun or a pronoun.

In the space below, write two sentences that contain adverb clauses, two that contain adjective clauses, and two that contain noun clauses.

95

Simple and Compound Sentences

A **simple sentence** contains one independent clause.

    Example: The dog is barking.

A simple sentence can have a compound subject and a compound verb.

A **compound sentence** contains two or more independent clauses.

    Example: The dog is barking, and it has been all afternoon.

Read the following sentences. Write **S** on the line if it is a simple sentence.

    Write **C** if it is a compound sentence.

____ 1.   Sean and Talisha are best friends.

____ 2.   I like to snowboard in the winter, and I like to skateboard in the summer.

____ 3.   Donald finished his test and handed it to his teacher.

____ 4.   You drive the car, and I'll walk.

____ 5.   Luis, Beatrix, and Rose all ran in the race.

____ 6.   I went to the mall first, and then I stopped at the grocery store.

96

Complex and Compound-Complex

A **complex sentence** contains one independent clause and one or more subordinate clauses.

> **Example:** Although I have been to the beach several times this week, I want to go again today.

A **compound-complex sentence** contains two or more independent clauses and one or more subordinate clauses.

> **Example:** If you are late for school today, you will miss your test, and you will probably get a detention.

Read the following sentences. Write **C** on the line for complex or **CC** on the line for compound-complex.

___ 1. I like cake a lot more than I like ice cream.

___ 2. Nicole went to school, but Dave stayed home because he had the flu.

___ 3. If you go see a movie, you have to take your brother, and he has to sit with you.

___ 4. Because you stayed home from school today, you cannot go out tonight.

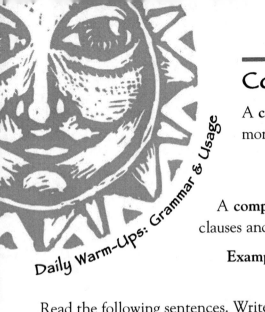

Daily Warm-Ups: Grammar & Usage

97

Clause Fragments

A fragment is not a complete sentence. It does not express a complete thought. Turn the following fragments into complete sentences. Write the sentence on the line.

1. I forgot your birthday. Because I didn't write it on my calendar.

   _____

2. Here is my history paper. That you wanted to read before I handed it in.

   _____

3. Grandma brought strawberry pie. Which was a big hit.

   _____

4. Since it is raining. We are going to the movies instead.

   _____

5. Where is Monica? Who was supposed to help me study.

   _____

98

Run-on Sentences

A **run-on sentence** is two or more sentences that are written as one sentence. Correct the following run-on sentences. Write the sentence on the line.

1. I broke my leg, the doctor took an X ray.

   _____

2. Kyle got a new laptop he uses it all the time.

   _____

3. Thanh went to bed early he wasn't feeling well.

   _____

4. Angela wrote a short story, she won an award for it.

   _____

5. Samantha got her license she practiced for hours the day before her test.

   _____

Daily Warm-Ups: Grammar & Usage

99

© 2006 Walch Publishing

Fragments and Run-ons

Create three sentence fragments and three run-on sentences.
Then exchange your sentences with a classmate and correct his
or her sentences.

100

Principal Parts

A verb has four principal parts: present, present participle, past, and past participle.

Present	walk
Present Participle	am walking
Past	walked
Past Participle	have walked

Choose a verb from the list below. Write the verb's four principal parts. Then use each of the parts in a sentence.

play   ask   stop   cook   bake

Daily Warm-Ups: Grammar & Usage

101

Regular Verbs

A **regular verb** is a verb that contains *-ed* or *-d* in its past and past participle forms. If you can add *-ed* or *-d* to the present form of the verb, it is a regular verb.

Think of five regular verbs, and use them to complete the following chart.

Daily Warm-Ups: Grammar & Usage

102

	Present	Present Participle	Past	Past Participle
1.				
2.				
3.				
4.				
5.				

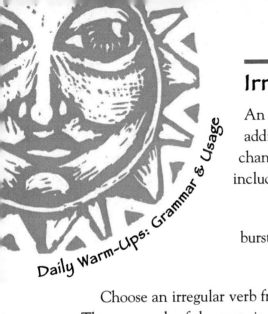

Irregular Verbs 1

An **irregular verb** cannot form its past and past participle by adding *-ed* or *-d* to its present form. Some irregular verbs do not change forms in the present, past, and past participle. These include the following verbs:

burst   cost   hit   let   put

Choose an irregular verb from the list above. Write the verb's four principal parts. Then use each of the parts in a sentence.

Daily Warm-Ups: Grammar & Usage

103

Irregular Verbs II

Remember that an **irregular verb** cannot form its past and past participle by adding *-ed* or *-d* to its present form. Some irregular verbs have the same form for the past and past participle. These verbs include the following:

bring   feel   fight   find   hold   leave   make   sell   win

Think of at least five other irregular verbs that follow this form. Use them to complete the chart below.

	Present	Present Participle	Past	Past Participle
1.				
2.				
3.				
4.				
5.				

Irregular Verbs III

Remember that an **irregular verb** cannot form its past and past participle by adding *-ed* or *-d* to its present form. Some irregular verbs form the past participle by adding *-n* to the past.

Present	break
Present Participle	breaking
Past	broke
Past Participle	broken

Think of another irregular verb that follows this pattern. Write its principal parts in a chart like the one above. Then use each of the principal parts in a sentence.

105

Daily Warm-Ups: Grammar & Usage

Irregular Verbs IV

Remember that an **irregular verb** cannot form its past and past participle by adding -*ed* or -*d* to its present form. Some irregular verbs form the past participle by adding -*n* to the present.

Present	see
Present Participle	seeing
Past	saw
Past Participle	seen

Circle the correct verb form to complete each sentence.

106

1. I have (grew, grown) several types of vegetables in my garden every summer.

2. The pitcher (threw, thrown) out the runner at first base.

3. She must have (know, known) that you were coming today.

4. The robbers (took, taken) all of my jewelry.

5. Please (give, gave) me your keys.

© 2006 Walch Publishing

Irregular Verbs V

Remember that an **irregular verb** cannot form its past and past participle by adding *-ed* or *-d* to its present form. Some irregular verbs form the past and past participle by changing a vowel. These include *begin, drink, shrink, sing, sink,* and *swim.* Complete the chart below with the principal parts of these six irregular verbs.

Present	Present Participle	Past	Past Participle
1. begin			
2. drink			
3. shrink			
4. sing			
5. sink			
6. swim			

107

Daily Warm-Ups: Grammar & Usage

Irregular Verbs VI

Remember that an **irregular verb** cannot form its past and past participle by adding *-ed* or *-d* to its present form.

Write the correct principal part on the line for each irregular verb in parentheses.

1. Where have they (go)? _____

2. The little boy (fall) out of the tree. _____

3. I have (ride) several of the horses at that stable. _____

4. We (eat) at that restaurant across the street. _____

5. I think I (wear) that yesterday. _____

6. We have (run) all over the city. _____

7. They (come) to the meeting a bit overdressed. _____

8. You have (write) one of the best essays in the class. _____

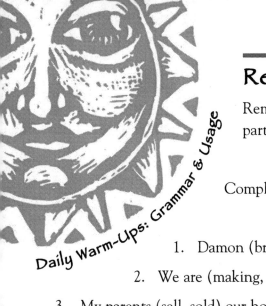

Reviewing Irregular Verbs 1

Remember that an **irregular verb** cannot form its past and past participle by adding *-ed* or *-d* to its present form.

Complete the following sentences by circling the correct verb form.

1. Damon (bring, brought) his sister to school.

2. We are (making, made) a cake for your birthday tonight.

3. My parents (sell, sold) our house after only a week on the market.

4. Please wait until I have (spoke, spoken).

5. The students (stole, stolen) the rival mascot.

6. Will you (draw, drew) me a map so I can find it?

7. I should have (knew, known) that you wouldn't make it to practice.

8. I (saw, seen) her down by the library.

109

Daily Warm-Ups: Grammar & Usage

Reviewing Irregular Verbs II

Remember that an **irregular verb** cannot form its past and past participle by adding *-ed* or *-d* to its present form.

Read the following sentences. If the verb is used correctly, write **C** on the line. If the verb is used incorrectly, write **I** on the line.

___ 1. Tristan finally brang his book to class today.

___ 2. We begun class early today.

___ 3. My contact lens must have sunk to the bottom of the pool.

___ 4. That chair must have broke when you sat on it.

___ 5. Have you seen Ms. Fecteau?

___ 6. Who taught the class last Monday?

___ 7. I have thought about majoring in psychology next year.

___ 8. When did you spoke to the guidance counselor?

110

Lay vs. Lie

Some verbs are easily confused. This includes the verbs *lay* and *lie*.
Lay means "to put or set down." *Lie* means "to rest or recline."

Present	Present Participle	Past	Past Participle
lay	laying	laid	laid
lie	lying	lay	lain

Read the following sentences. Write **C** on the line if the underlined verb is used correctly. Write **I** on the line if it is used incorrectly.

____ 1. I want to <u>lie</u> on the couch after dinner.

____ 2. <u>Lie</u> your books on the floor while taking the exam.

____ 3. They are <u>lying</u> out on the beach.

____ 4. I <u>laid</u> down for a nap just in time.

____ 5. Please <u>lay</u> your pencils down and close your books.

111

Verb Usage

Sit vs. Set

Sit and *set* are two other verbs that are easily confused. *Sit* means
"to rest in an upright position." *Set* means "to put or place."

Present	Present Participle	Past	Past Participle
sit	sitting	sat	sat
set	setting	set	set

Complete the following sentences with the correct form of *sit* or *set*.

1. Please _____ down at your desks.

2. We are _____ the table for dinner.

3. We are _____ at the table for dinner.

4. The salad is _____ over there on the counter.

5. We have _____ here for a long time.

6. The sun _____ around 8:00 P.M. this time of year.

Daily Warm-Ups: Grammar & Usage

© 2006 Walch Publishing

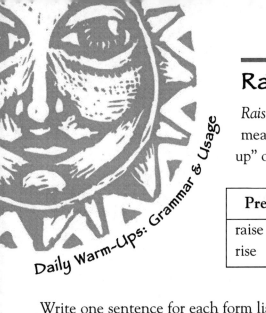

Raise vs. Rise

Raise and *rise* are two other verbs that are easily confused. *Raise* means "to lift up," "to increase," or "to grow." *Rise* means "to get up" or "to move upward."

Present	Present Participle	Past	Past Participle
raise	raising	raised	raised
rise	rising	rose	risen

Write one sentence for each form listed in the chart above.

Verb Tenses I

The **tense** of a verb is the time expressed by that verb. A verb has six tenses: present, past, future, present perfect, past perfect, and future perfect. Look at the tenses of the verb *play* below.

Present	play
Past	played
Future	will play
Present Perfect	have played
Past Perfect	had played
Future Perfect	will have played

Study the chart above. Then create your own chart for the verb *call*.

114

Verb Tenses II

Remember that the **tense** of a verb is the time expressed by that verb. Complete the following chart for the verb *cook*.

Present	
Past	
Future	
Present Perfect	
Past Perfect	
Future Perfect	

Now use each of the verb tenses you listed in the chart above in sentences of your own.

Daily Warm-Ups: Grammar & Usage

115

Verb Tenses III

Remember that the **tense** of a verb is the time expressed by that verb. The tenses of an irregular verb are a bit trickier to form. Knowing the four principal parts of the irregular verb will help you. Look at the four principal parts of the verb *bring*.

Present	bring
Present Participle	bringing
Past	brought
Past Participle	have brought

Now look at the six tenses of *bring*.

Present	bring
Past	brought
Future	will bring
Present Perfect	have brought
Past Perfect	had brought
Future Perfect	will have brought

Now create two charts like the ones above for the irregular verb *drive*.

116

Verb Tenses IV

Explain how each tense listed below is formed.

1. past tense _____

   _____

2. future tense _____

   _____

3. present perfect tense _____

   _____

4. past perfect tense _____

   _____

5. future perfect tense _____

   _____

117

Verb Tenses V

Read the following sentences. Write the tense of the bold verb form on the line after each sentence.

1. I **will have made** at least twenty phone calls by the end of the day. _____

2. I **have used** the treadmill a lot this week. _____

3. I **will do** my homework later. _____

4. I **have eaten** a sandwich every day for lunch this week. _____

5. They **had taken** the baby to the pediatrician. _____

6. I **run** at least three times a week. _____

118

Progressive Forms

Progressive forms of verbs express ongoing action and usually end in *-ing*. Like all verbs, progressive forms have six tenses.

Present Progressive	I am running.
Past Progressive	I was running.
Future Progressive	I will be running.
Present Perfect Progressive	I have been running.
Past Perfect Progressive	I had been running.
Future Perfect Progressive	I will have been running.

Write a sentence for each progressive tense of the verb *travel*.

Daily Warm-Ups: Grammar & Usage

119

Emphatic Forms

Emphatic forms are used to show emphasis. They appear in two tenses: present emphatic and past emphatic. Present emphatic tenses include the word *do* or *does* before the verb. Past emphatic tenses include the word *did* before the verb.

> **Examples:** I **do run** every day. (present emphatic)
>
> I **did run** yesterday. (past emphatic)

Write six sentences that express the emphatic form. Three should contain the present emphatic, and three should contain the past emphatic.

120

Active and Passive Voice

When a sentence is written in the **active voice,** it means that the subject is performing the action. When a sentence is written in the **passive voice,** it means that the action of the verb is being performed on the subject.

Examples: Olivia wrote the essay. (active)

The essay was written by Olivia. (passive)

Daily Warm-Ups: Grammar & Usage

Read the following sentences. Write **A** on the line if it is written in active voice. Write **P** on the line if it is written in passive voice.

____ 1. The house was cleaned by the cleaning lady.

____ 2. Keiko filled out her college applications.

____ 3. The lifeguard saved the drowning toddler's life.

____ 4. The computer was fixed by Justin.

____ 5. Sam was bitten by the dog.

____ 6. The dog bit Sam.

121

Agreement I

A verb must agree with its subject in number. The number of the subject is either singular or plural. Nouns are made plural by adding -s or -es in most cases. Singular and plural pronouns are:

Singular: I, you, he, she, it   **Plural:** we, you, they

Verbs are also singular and plural. A singular verb must be paired with a singular subject. A plural verb must be paired with a plural subject.

Rewrite each sentence below with the correct agreement.

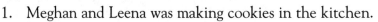

1. Meghan and Leena was making cookies in the kitchen.

   _____

2. Cesar have a lot of homework tonight.

   _____

3. You and I am going to practice, right?

   _____

4. The band play downtown every weekend.

   _____

122

Agreement II

Remember that subjects and verbs must agree in number. Singular verbs should follow the words *each, neither, everyone, everybody, nobody,* and *someone.*

Read the following sentences. Write a check mark next to those that are in agreement.

___ 1. Everyone in the choir practice after school.

___ 2. Someone must really love me.

___ 3. Neither of us are going to the party this weekend.

___ 4. Nobody likes a cheater.

___ 5. Each of you have taken this exam.

___ 6. Everybody in the class pass in the homework on time.

___ 7. Has nobody seen the new reality show on Channel 6?

___ 8. Neither of you were at the assembly this morning.

Daily Warm-Ups: Grammar & Usage

Agreement III

Remember that subjects and verbs must agree in number. Plural verbs almost always follow the words *all*, *both*, *few*, *many*, *several*, and *some*.

Write six sentences that each use one of the words listed above. Make sure they are followed by a plural verb. Then exchange your sentences with a classmate and make sure his or her sentences are in agreement.

Daily Warm-Ups: Grammar & Usage

124

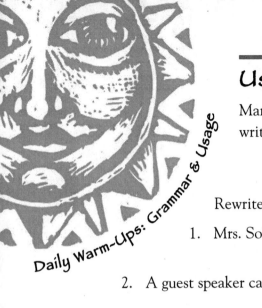

Using Better Verbs

Many verbs are boring and overused. You can greatly improve your writing by using more colorful verbs.

Examples: Russ **came** into class just as the bell rang.

Russ **raced** into class just as the bell rang.

Rewrite each of the following sentences using more colorful verbs.

1. Mrs. Solis went to the back of the classroom.

2. A guest speaker came to our class yesterday.

3. Please go to the board and write your answer.

4. The dog entered the house.

5. Where did you put my book?

125

Pronoun Cases

Pronouns come in three cases: nominative, objective, and possessive. Pronoun forms in the nominative case are listed below.

Nominative Case	
Singular	I, you, he, she, it
Plural	we, you, they

Complete the pronoun charts below for the objective and possessive cases.

126

Objective Case
Singular
Plural

Possessive Case
Singular
Plural

Nominative Case

The **nominative case** is used for subjects and predicate nominatives. These pronouns are *I*, *you*, *he*, *she*, *it*, *we*, and *they*.

Read the following sentences. Circle the pronoun that correctly completes each sentence.

1. Troy and (I, me) are going for a run after school.

2. (We, Us) want to get in shape for track season.

3. That was (she, her) on the phone.

4. Sadie is an excellent painter. The winner of the art contest was (her, she).

5. (He, Him) and Grant are going on a tour of the museum.

6. The class marshals will be Layla and (I, me).

7. You and (I, me) should work on our project this afternoon.

8. The students on the basketball team are (they, them).

127

© 2006 Walch Publishing

Objective Case

The **objective case** pronouns are used for direct objects, indirect objects, and objects of a preposition. These pronouns include *me, you, him, her, it, us,* and *them.*

Read the following sentences. Put a check mark next to those that contain the correct pronouns.

_____ 1. Abigail told we to meet her in the gym.

_____ 2. Please bring Anna and me to the movies tonight.

_____ 3. Did you ask your mother and I?

_____ 4. Show he what you learned today.

_____ 5. Will you go with me tonight?

_____ 6. Lamont drives Barbara and I crazy.

_____ 7. The competition came down to he and I.

_____ 8. We are having dinner with them tonight.

128

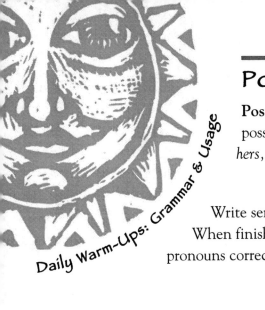

Possessive Case

Possessive case pronouns are used to show ownership or possession. These pronouns include *my, mine, your, yours, his, her, hers, its, our, ours, their,* and *theirs.*

Write sentences that use each of the possessive pronouns listed above. When finished, check your sentences to be sure that you have used the pronouns correctly.

Daily Warm-Ups: Grammar & Usage

129

Who and Whom

The pronouns *who* and *whom* are often confused. *Who* is used when someone is the subject. *Whom* is used when someone is the object of a verb or preposition.

Read the following sentences. Circle the correct pronoun to complete each sentence.

1. The teacher (who, whom) gave us our notes is Mr. Chin.

2. To (who, whom) do you want to send this e-mail?

3. (Who, Whom) will be at the assembly?

4. (Who, Whom) did you ask for help?

5. About (who, whom) are you speaking?

6. I don't know (who, whom) the instructor is.

7. Mr. Alexander, (who, whom) is my favorite teacher, returned our quizzes.

8. Carly is the woman to (who, whom) you address your questions.

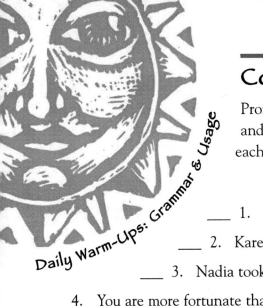

Daily Warm-Ups: Grammar & Usage

Comparison Pronouns

Pronouns are often used in comparisons following the words *than* and *as*. Read the following sentences. Put a check mark next to each sentence that correctly uses pronouns in comparisons.

___ 1. My sister is taller than me.

___ 2. Kareem works as hard as they.

___ 3. Nadia took as long as me to read the book.

___ 4. You are more fortunate than I.

___ 5. You look better than him in the picture.

___ 6. They swam faster than he in the race.

___ 7. Mr. Muñoz said everyone did as well as me.

___ 8. Clayton knew that he could do better than her.

131

© 2006 Walch Publishing

Antecedents 1

A pronoun must agree in number and gender with its antecedent. Recall that an antecedent is the word that the pronoun replaces or refers to.

For each of the following antecedents, write a sentence with a pronoun that agrees in number and gender.

1. student _____

   _____

2. students _____

   _____

3. everyone _____

   _____

4. some _____

   _____

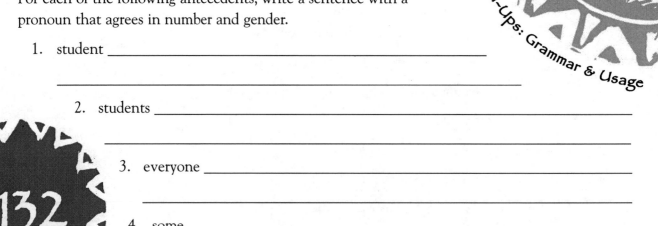

Daily Warm-Ups: Grammar & Usage

132

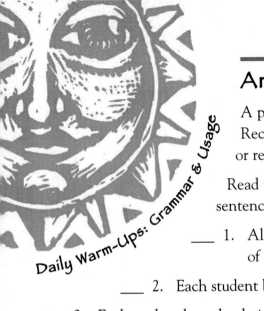

Antecedents II

A pronoun must agree in number and gender with its antecedent. Recall that an antecedent is the word that the pronoun replaces or refers to.

Read the following sentences. Put a check mark next to the sentences that have pronoun/antecedent agreement.

___ 1. All students should report to the office for their first day of orientation.

___ 2. Each student brought his or her textbook to class.

___ 3. Each student brought their textbooks to class.

___ 4. Either Lauren or Mina will ride their bike to school.

___ 5. Both of my children got their acceptance letters today.

Now write two sentences of your own using pronouns that agree with their antecedents.

133

© 2006 Walch Publishing

Pronoun Review 1

Write a paragraph about what you hope to accomplish in the next year. Label all pronouns in the nominative case with **NC.** Label all pronouns in the objective case with **OC.** Label the pronouns in the possessive case with **PC.**

Daily Warm-Ups: Grammar & Usage

134

Pronoun Review II

Take out an essay or paper that you have written this year. Underline all the pronouns. Check to see if you used them correctly. Did you use the pronoun cases correctly? Do the pronouns agree with their antecedents? After you evaluate your paper, write a paragraph in the space below explaining your understanding of pronouns. Has your understanding changed since you wrote the paper?

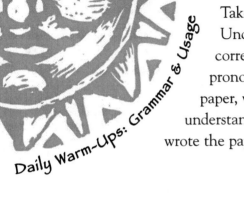

Daily Warm-Ups: Grammar & Usage

135

Comparisons 1

Adjectives can be used in comparisons. This means that the form of the adjective changes depending on how many things are being compared. There are three degrees of comparison: positive, comparative, and superlative.

Examples: great (positive)
greater (comparative)
greatest (superlative)

The positive degree is used when no comparison is being made. Most comparatives, which compare two things, are formed by adding *-er* to the positive. Most superlatives, which compare more than two things, are formed by adding *-est* to the positive.

Write the comparative and superlative forms for each of the words below.

1. young _____   _____

2. bright _____   _____

3. quiet _____   _____

4. nice _____   _____

136

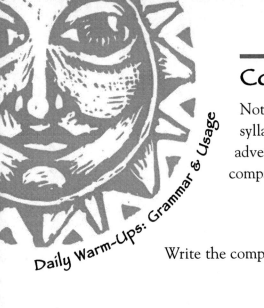

Comparisons II

Not all comparisons are created by adding *-er* and *-est*. Many two-syllable adjectives and adverbs and almost all adjectives and adverbs with three or more syllables use *more* or *most* to form comparatives and superlatives.

Examples: difficult, more difficult, most difficult

Write the comparative and superlative forms for each of the words below.

1. interesting _____ _____

2. small _____ _____

3. delicious _____ _____

4. funny _____ _____

5. friendly _____ _____

6. careful _____ _____

Daily Warm-Ups: Grammar & Usage

137

© 2006 Walch Publishing

Comparisons III

Some words are irregular in their comparative and superlative forms. Complete the chart below.

138

Positive	Comparative	Superlative
1. bad		
2. good		
3. many		
4. little		
5. much		

Comparisons IV

Recall that some comparatives and superlatives are formed by adding *-er* and *-est* to the adjective or adverb. Others are formed by putting the word *more* or *most* in front of the adjective or adverb. Other forms are irregular.

Read the following sentences. Circle the comparative or superlative that best completes each sentence.

1. This is the (more delicious, most delicious) apple pie I have ever tasted!

2. I am (better, best) at checkers than you are.

3. Today's sunset is (more beautiful, most beautiful) than yesterday's.

4. This dog is the (friendliest, most friendliest) dog in the neighborhood.

5. Angelo is the (taller, more taller) of the two brothers.

6. Your steak looks (tougher, more tough) than mine.

139

Daily Warm-Ups: Grammar & Usage

Comparisons V

Recall that some comparatives and superlatives are formed by adding *-er* and *-est* to the adjective or adverb. Others are formed by putting the word *more* or *most* in front of the adjective or adverb. Other forms are irregular.

For each of the words below, write a sentence using its comparative or superlative form.

1. bad _____

2. many _____

3. tasty _____

4. different _____

5. intelligent _____

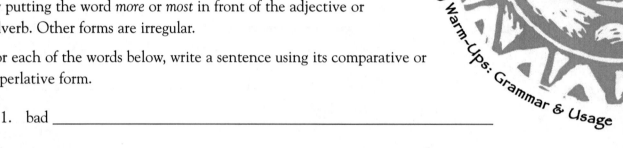

Comparisons VI

Remember that some comparatives and superlatives are formed by adding *-er* and *-est* to the adjective or adverb. Others are formed by putting the word *more* or *most* in front of the adjective or adverb. Other forms are irregular.

Advertisements often use comparisons to convince consumers that they should use the product or service. Use your knowledge of comparatives and superlatives to write an ad for a business of your choice. Your ad can be a visual ad found in a newspaper or magazine or on the Internet. Or you can write a script for a television or radio ad. Be sure to use at least five comparatives and superlatives.

Daily Warm-Ups: Grammar & Usage

141

Good and Well 1

The words *good* and *well* are often used incorrectly. *Good* is always an adjective. *Well* is usually an adverb, but when it means "attractive" or "in good health," it is an adjective.

Read the following sentences. Circle the word that best completes each sentence.

1. I was absent yesterday because I didn't feel (good, well).

2. You did a (good, well) job raking the lawn.

3. Eric, you don't look (good, well). Do you want to go see the nurse?

4. I didn't do very (good, well) on that quiz.

5. That's a (good, well) way to do it.

6. Melanie plays (good, well) after a (good, well) night's rest.

142

Good and Well II

Remember that *good* is always an adjective. *Well* is usually an adverb, but when it means "attractive" or "in good health," it is an adjective.

Write six sentences in the space below. Write three that use *good* and three that use *well*.

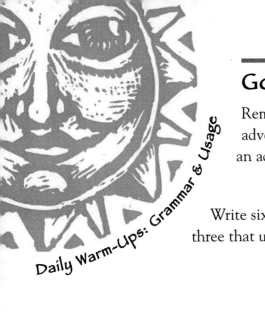

143

Double Negatives

A **negative** is a word that means "no." Common negatives include *barely, hardly, never, no, nobody, none, not, nothing,* and *scarcely.* Using a negative word can change the meaning of the sentence. Using two negative words causes the negatives to cancel each other out, leaving the sentence with a positive meaning.

Read the following sentences. Rewrite those that contain double negatives so that they contain only one negative.

1. You don't need no shoes.

2. We never catch nothing when we go fishing.

3. Nobody ignored the fire alarm when it sounded.

4. We didn't have none of the new uniforms for our game.

5. There's hardly any time left for questions.

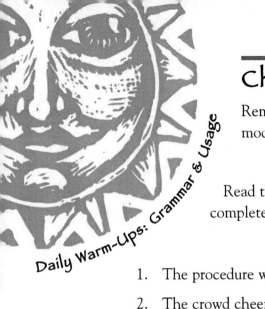

Choosing Adjectives and Adverbs

Remember that adjectives modify nouns and pronouns. Adverbs modify verbs, adjectives, and other adverbs.

Read the following sentences. Circle the adjective or adverb that best completes each sentence.

1. The procedure was (quick, quickly) and painless.

2. The crowd cheered (loud, loudly) for the home team.

3. I ran (slow, slowly) back to my car.

4. The students were (eager, eagerly) to get out of class.

5. Vincent (nervous, nervously) tapped his pencil on the desk.

6. Jonah was (proud, proudly) of his artwork.

Daily Warm-Ups: Grammar & Usage

145

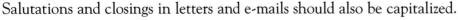

First Words and *I*

The first word of a sentence or a line of poetry should be capitalized. The pronoun *I* should also be capitalized.

> **Example:** That is the first thing **I** do when **I** wake up in the morning.

Salutations and closings in letters and e-mails should also be capitalized.

> **Example:** Dear Zahara, Sincerely

Write an e-mail in the space below about what you did last night. Be sure to capitalize correctly.

Daily Warm-Ups: Grammar & Usage

146

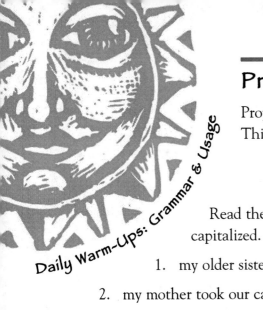

Proper Nouns

Proper nouns and their abbreviations should always be capitalized. This includes names of people and names of pets.

Examples: **A**iden O'**C**onnor, my dog **B**uster

Read the following sentences. Circle the letters that should be capitalized.

1. my older sister, amy, and i went out to dinner on my birthday.

2. my mother took our cat, bentley, to the veterinarian.

3. ashok used mom's car to pick up kenny.

4. should i go with the russells to soccer practice?

5. irina and i baked a cake for elizabeth's party.

Now write two sentences of your own about two of your friends. Be sure to use proper capitalization.

147

© 2006 Walch Publishing

Daily Warm-Ups: Grammar & Usage

Geographical Names

Geographical names should be capitalized. These include the following:

towns/cities	islands	continents
countries	streets	mountains
world regions	counties	bodies of water
stars/planets	states	

For each type of geographical name listed in the box above, write an example below. Be sure to capitalize correctly.

148

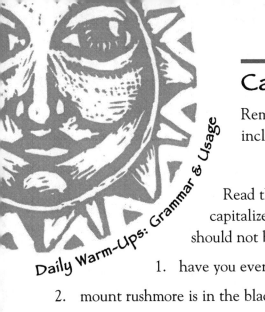

Capitalizing Proper Nouns

Remember that proper nouns should always be capitalized. These include names of people and animals and geographical names.

Read the following sentences. Circle the letters that should be capitalized. Draw a line through any letters that are capitalized but should not be.

1. have you ever been to mount rushmore?

2. mount rushmore is in the black hills of south dakota.

3. we visited the amazing sight last Summer.

4. we drove through the midwest to get there.

5. we traveled there in a van with the garcias.

6. their children are the same age as we are.

7. on our way there and back, we crossed the mississippi river.

8. next summer we're going to the grand canyon.

Daily Warm-Ups: Grammar & Usage

Groups, Time Periods, and Events

Names of groups should be capitalized. These include organizations, businesses, institutions, government agencies, political parties, and teams.

Examples: United Nations, Harvard University, Republican Party, Chicago Bears

Time periods and events are also capitalized. These include days, months, holidays, historical events, historical periods, important documents, and special events.

Examples: Sunday, January, Flag Day, World War II, the Bill of Rights, the Olympics

150

Give an example of each type of group, time period, and event listed above. Make sure to capitalize correctly.

Nationalities, Races, and Religions

Nationalities, races, religions, and languages should be capitalized.

Examples: China, Asian, Judaism, French

Write a paragraph about a foreign country. Include information about race, common religions, languages, and geographical names and features. Be sure to capitalize correctly.

Daily Warm-Ups: Grammar & Usage

151

© 2006 Walch Publishing

Capitalizing Other Proper Nouns

Many other proper nouns should be capitalized. These include awards, brand names, bridges and buildings, memorials and monuments, vehicles such as ships and space shuttles, names of academic courses, and technological terms.

Examples: Nobel Prize, Kleenex, Sears Tower, Lincoln Memorial, *Challenger*, Algebra I, Internet

Daily Warm-Ups: Grammar & Usage

Read the list of nouns below. Write a check mark next to those that should be capitalized.

152

___ 1. first prize

___ 2. brooklyn bridge

___ 3. band-aid

___ 4. computer

___ 5. empire state building

___ 6. high school

___ 7. biology I

___ 8. world wide web

___ 9. callahan tunnel

___10. space shuttle

Proper Adjectives

Most proper adjectives and compound adjectives are capitalized.

Examples: French fries, African American

Read the following sentences. Circle the letters that should be capitalized. Draw a line through any letters that are capitalized but should not be.

1. my Mother is french canadian.

2. we had sweet italian sausage for dinner.

3. our dog is a german shepherd named hans.

4. the neighbors have an irish setter that plays with hans.

5. carlos brought swiss chocolates back from europe.

6. Dad bought alaskan king crab at the Seafood Market.

7. i am part american indian.

8. you have a strong british accent.

Daily Warm-Ups: Grammar & Usage

153

Titles of People

Titles of people should be capitalized in certain situations.

> **Examples:** Governor Randolph, President Bush, Aunt
> Hilda, Mom

Titles can be confusing because they are not always capitalized.

> **Examples:** the governor, my aunt, your mom

Read the following sentences. Circle the letters that should be capitalized. Draw a line through any letters that are capitalized but should not be.

154

1. have you seen coach hancock?

2. it was grandma who baked the cookies.

3. my mom will bring my uniform before the game.

4. the man on television is going to be our new Senator.

5. auntie, will you help me?

6. i didn't know you were Matthew's Father.

Titles of Written and Other Works

Titles of written works should be capitalized. These include books, chapters, short stories, poems, newspapers, articles, and magazines. Also capitalized are titles of plays, television programs, movies, and works of art. Prepositions and articles within the title should not be capitalized unless they are the first or last words.

Examples: *The Catcher in the Rye*, "Stopping by Woods on a Snowy Evening," *American Idol*

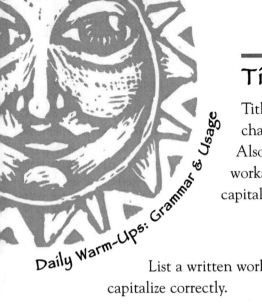

Daily Warm-Ups: Grammar & Usage

List a written work for each of the following categories. Be sure to capitalize correctly.

1. favorite book _____

2. favorite short story _____

3. popular newspaper _____

4. favorite magazine _____

5. favorite play _____

6. favorite television series _____

155

Capitalization Review 1

Read the following sentences. Correct any words that need to be capitalized. Some words may be capitalized that should not be. Draw a line through each letter that is incorrectly capitalized.

Daily Warm-Ups: Grammar & Usage

1. someday i want to climb Mount washington.

2. my Dad said he would help me buy the car that's for sale down the Street, but I don't want a volkswagen jetta.

3. on september 18, i will be eighteen years old.

4. my favorite teacher is mrs. kennedy. she teaches english.

5. on our trip to california, we went to the san diego Zoo.

6. our house is just down the street from yours at 349 wallingford way.

7. this Summer i want to go see the boston red sox at Fenway park.

8. my Grandmother is irish, and my Grandfather is italian.

156

Capitalization Review II

Write the following items on the lines. Correct any capitalization errors. Write *correct* on the line if there are no errors.

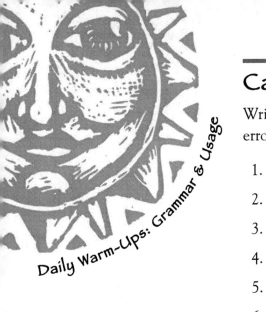

Daily Warm-Ups: Grammar & Usage

1. the civil war _____

2. my Dad _____

3. labor day in september _____

4. lake erie _____

5. the Governor of indiana _____

6. the boston globe _____

7. my brother martin _____

8. elementary school _____

9. algebra I and geometry _____

10. summer in maine _____

11. the democratic party _____

12. visit the Northeast _____

157

Capitalization Review III

Write a sentence for each of the following topics. Be sure to capitalize correctly.

1. football team _____

2. favorite place to visit _____

3. your heritage _____

4. your state's governor _____

5. a brand name _____

6. your favorite movie _____

7. a holiday memory _____

8. a region of the United States _____

9. a family member _____

10. the street your school is on _____

158

Capitalization Review IV

Write a check mark next to the sentences that are capitalized correctly.

____ 1. My Mother said she would rent *Lord of the Rings* for us this weekend.

____ 2. We found several artifacts from World War II at the museum.

____ 3. I think you should take Elm street to the theater.

____ 4. My favorite Shakespeare play is *Romeo And Juliet*.

____ 5. I will attend Dickinson College in Pennsylvania next fall.

____ 6. We will travel throughout the midwest this Summer.

____ 7. Thanksgiving always falls on the third Thursday in November.

____ 8. My Aunt Millie's apartment is just South of Boston.

____ 9. Even though Dad is a Republican, he's voting for the Democratic Party candidate.

____ 10. Grammy hayes will pick you up out front. She'll be in the Cadillac.

Daily Warm-Ups: Grammar & Usage

159

Capitalization Review V

List as many rules for capitalization as you can in the space below. You should be able to think of at least twenty. Review your list with a classmate to see what you are missing.

160

End Marks

Sentences can end with periods, question marks, or exclamation points. This depends on the type of sentence. A **declarative sentence (DS)** makes a statement and ends with a period. An **imperative sentence (IM)** makes a request or gives a direction or command and ends with a period or an exclamation point. An **interrogative sentence (IN)** asks a question and ends with a question mark. An **exclamatory sentence (ES)** expresses strong emotion and ends with an exclamation point.

Read the following sentences and add the correct end punctuation. Using the letters in parentheses above, write the type of sentence on the line.

____ 1. Where have you been

____ 2. Ouch That hurts

____ 3. My neighbor gave me a ride to school

____ 4. Take the cat off the counter

____ 5. Please bring your books to class on Monday

Daily Warm-Ups: Grammar & Usage

161

Periods in Abbreviations

Periods are used at the ends of sentences. Periods are also used at the end of abbreviations.

> **Examples:** Mrs., Dr., Ulysses S. Grant, A.M., P.M., Ave., Rd., Inc.

List as many abbreviations that use periods as you can in the space below.

Now use five of the abbreviations you listed above in sentences.

162

Bonus: What abbreviations do not use periods?

Commas in a Series

Commas are used to help avoid confusion in sentences. They separate items, and they enclose items. Commas are often used to separate items in a series.

> **Example:** The fruit salad has cantaloupe, grapes, pineapple, honeydew, and watermelon in it.

Read the following sentences. Add any necessary commas, and cross out any that are unnecessary.

1. I will attend, Boston College, the University of Massachusetts, or Harvard.

2. My mother my father and my sister all went to Boston College.

3. My friends are attending colleges in California, Colorado and Florida.

4. What college I attend depends on what I get for financial aid what scholarships I am awarded and how much money my parents can contribute.

5. I am excited about college, but first I have to, be accepted, complete my senior project, and graduate from high school.

163

© 2006 Walch Publishing

Commas Between Two Adjectives

Sometimes commas should separate two adjectives that precede a noun. You can tell if the comma is necessary by putting the word *and* between the adjectives. If the sentence still makes sense, a comma is necessary. If the sentence does not make sense, the comma should be omitted. Usually commas are unnecessary after numbers or adjectives that refer to size, shape, or age.

Daily Warm-Ups: Grammar & Usage

Examples: Make sure you bring that big yellow umbrella. ("Big *and* yellow umbrella" doesn't make sense.)

Make sure you bring that old, worn-out umbrella. ("Old *and* worn-out umbrella" makes sense.)

Read the following sentences. If a comma should be inserted between the adjectives, write **C** on the line. Write **N** if no comma is necessary.

164

____ 1. Emily left three short messages on our voice mail at home.

____ 2. The hot humid weather should be here by the end of the month.

____ 3. You've had those old dirty sneakers since middle school.

____ 4. That baby has the most beautiful bright blue eyes.

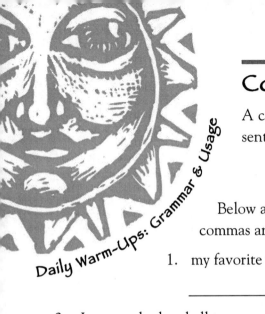

Commas in Compound Sentences

A comma is necessary to separate two independent clauses in a sentence if the clauses are joined by a conjunction.

Example: My family went to Florida, and Sayeed's family went to California.

Below are pairs of independent clauses. Put each pair together using commas and conjunctions.

1. my favorite fruit is watermelon   my sister's favorite is kiwi

_____

2. I am on the baseball team   Kendra is on the track team

_____

3. Billy rode his bike   his mother walked the dog

_____

4. Tawana put up the tent   Jacob built a fire

_____

Daily Warm-Ups: Grammar & Usage

165

Commas and Introductory Elements

A comma is necessary after introductory elements such as prepositional phrases, participial phrases, and adverb clauses.

Prepositional phrase: After we went to dinner, we saw a movie.

Participial phrase: Walking by the classroom, I noticed we had a substitute.

Adverb clause: Because I was running late, I needed a ride to school.

Read the following sentences. Add a comma when necessary.

1. If you want to go to the concert you have to get tickets immediately.

2. In 2001 terrorists flew planes into the World Trade Center.

3. Listening to the lecture I realized I left my notes at home.

4. Under several stacks of paper I found my application.

5. Since you weren't here yesterday we decided to do the presentation without you.

166

Daily Warm-Ups: Grammar & Usage

Commas in Dates, Addresses, and Letters

Commas are used to separate parts of dates and addresses.

Examples: On June 3, 2006, my sister graduated from high school.

We live at 442 Camden Lane, Chestnut Hill, Connecticut 06226.

Daily Warm-Ups: Grammar & Usage

Commas are also used in letters and e-mails after salutations and closings.

Examples: Dear Mrs. Rodriguez,   Love,   Sincerely,

Imagine you are setting up an interview for a scholarship. E-mail the person who will be interviewing you. Tell him or her where you live and when you will be available for an interview. Be sure to use commas correctly.

167

Commas in Direct Address and Parenthetical Expressions

Commas are used in direct address.

> **Example: Jade,** have you heard about the game?

Commas are also used in parenthetical expressions. This is information in the sentence that can be taken out without changing the meaning.

> **Example: By the way,** do you have any extra gym clothes?

Read the following sentences and add commas when necessary.

1. The teachers I believe are all in a meeting.

2. Where Mr. Beckett do you suggest I write my reply?

3. To tell you the truth Leah I've never heard of anything like that.

4. This car on the other hand seems as though it will suit your needs.

5. Kristy please hand me the remote.

6. I do however think I can finish my essay by tomorrow.

168

Daily Warm-Ups: Grammar & Usage

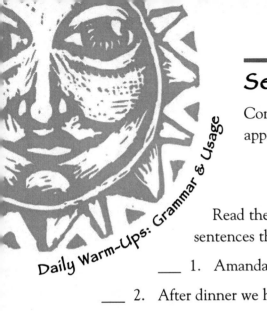

Setting Off Appositives

Commas are used to set off appositives. Remember that an appositive identifies or explains a noun or pronoun in a sentence.

Example: Henry, the boy I babysit, takes a long nap in the afternoon.

Read the following sentences. Write a check mark next to the sentences that have commas in the correct places.

___ 1. Amanda my best friend is leaving for college next week.

___ 2. After dinner we had dessert, something we haven't had in a long time.

___ 3. Kelisha, our team's leading scorer, will be out for the rest of the season.

___ 4. Mrs. Simmons my favorite teacher never gives homework over the weekend.

___ 5. John, my cousin, writes a column for the school newspaper.

___ 6. Belle the best dancer in the class has won many competitions.

___ 7. Mr. Menendez the lab assistant helped us write our reports.

___ 8. Sydney, typically a loner, ate her lunch with a classmate today.

169

Put In the Punctuation

In the space below, write a paragraph about your morning, but do not include any end marks or commas. Exchange paragraphs with a classmate. Insert any punctuation necessary in your classmate's paragraph. Then return the paragraphs. Check to see if your classmate inserted the proper punctuation in your paragraph.

Daily Warm-Ups: Grammar & Usage

170

Comma Rules

You have just spent some time reviewing commas. Think of all the rules for when commas are needed. List as many as you can below. You should be able to think of at least ten.

171

© 2006 Walch Publishing

Italics and Quotation Marks

Italics are used for most titles. These include books, magazines, newspapers, plays, movies, television programs, long musical compositions, works of art, and names of vehicles such as ships and space shuttles. Quotation marks are also used for titles. These include chapters in books, poems in books, articles in magazines or newspapers, episodes of television series, and songs.

Read the following sentences. Underline anything that should be in italics, and insert quotation marks where appropriate.

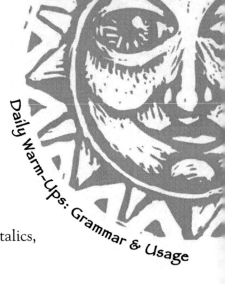

1. We have to recite Frost's Stopping by Woods on a Snowy Evening.

2. When I was younger, my favorite book was Tuck Everlasting.

3. I love almost all Disney movies, but my favorite is The Little Mermaid.

4. That was a wonderful rendition of America the Beautiful.

5. My father reads the Wall Street Journal every morning.

6. One of my favorite episodes of Friends was The One Where Everybody Finds Out.

Inserting Quotation Marks

Read the following sentences. You will notice that the quotation marks have been omitted. Insert the quotation marks when needed.

1. Hannah, have you read Maya Angelou's poem Phenomenal Woman? Mr. Harrison asked.

2. Your father said that he will drop you off at school on his way to work.

3. That building over there, he said, is the tallest building in the city.

4. Did you hear your grandmother say happy birthday?

5. I think the chapter titled The Ghost Returns is the scariest part of this novel.

6. Our history teacher told us that he wouldn't give us homework this weekend.

173

© 2006 Walch Publishing

Apostrophes

Apostrophes are most commonly used to show possession and in contractions.

      Examples: Is that **Dad's** car? (possession)

                No, that **isn't** his car. (contraction for *is not*)

Use apostrophes to turn the following words into possessives.

1. Simon _____
2. women _____
3. everyone _____
4. players _____
5. Travis _____
6. sister-in-law _____

Turn the following pairs of words into contractions and use each in a sentence.

7. cannot
8. he is
9. they are
10. you would

174

Semicolons

Semicolons are used between clauses of a compound sentence that are not joined by a conjunction. Semicolons also help avoid confusion.

Read the following sentences. If the semicolons are used correctly, write **C** on the line. If they are used incorrectly, write **I** on the line.

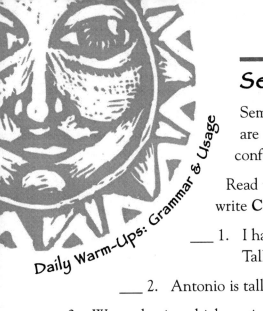

____ 1. I have never been to Boise, Idaho; Sacramento, California; or Tallahassee, Florida.

____ 2. Antonio is tall, Stacy is short.

____ 3. We are having chicken, rice, and salad for dinner; so don't spoil your appetite.

____ 4. Esther plays in a band; Kayla plays solo.

____ 5. I brought the graham crackers, marshmallows, and chocolate; you go in the woods and get sticks.

____ 6. Running inside with scissors; Bill could have hurt himself.

175

Colons

Colons are used before most lists. Often the colon is preceded by the words *the following*. Colons are also used to introduce long quotations. They are used between hours and minutes in time, between titles and subtitles, and after salutations in business letters.

Write five sentences about how you spend your weekends. You must use at least one colon in each sentence.

176

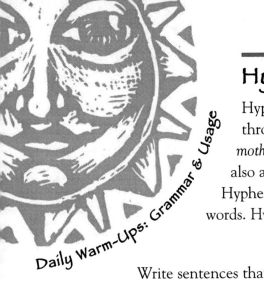

Hyphens

Hyphens are used when writing out the numbers twenty-one through ninety-nine. They are used in compound nouns such as *mother-in-law* and compound adjectives such as *all-around*. Hyphens also appear in fractions when the fractions are used as adjectives. Hyphens separate the prefixes *ex-*, *self-*, and *all-* from their base words. Hyphens also separate prefixes from proper nouns and adjectives.

Write sentences that include each of the following uses of hyphens.

1. numbers _____

2. compound nouns _____

3. compound adjectives _____

4. fractions _____

5. prefixes _____

Daily Warm-Ups: Grammar & Usage

177

Dashes and Parentheses

Dashes and parentheses work to set off information much as commas do. Dashes set off an abrupt change in thought, an appositive that is introduced by words such as *for example* and *for instance,* and parenthetical expressions or appositives that include commas. Parentheses are used to set off information that is not closely related to the meaning of the sentence.

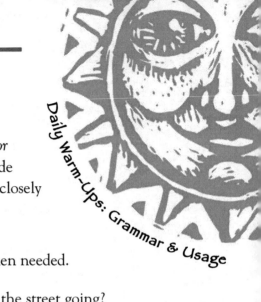

Read the following sentences. Insert dashes and parentheses when needed.

1. Where is the girl she just moved in across the street going?

2. We walked or should I say crawled back to our hotel room after a long day.

3. Three teachers Mr. Dugan, Ms. Ortiz, and Ms. Thayer are all nominated for the Teacher of the Year award.

4. That puppy often found sleeping in his cage bites my fingers when he plays.

Now write two sentences of your own. One should contain dashes, and one should contain parentheses.

Punctuation Review I

Read each of the following sentences, paying close attention to the punctuation. If the punctuation is correct, write **C** on the line. If it is incorrect, write **I** on the line and correct the punctuation errors.

Daily Warm-Ups: Grammar & Usage

____ 1. Isn't your application due Monday, May 1 by 12:00 A.M.?

____ 2. Out of all twenty-one of you, only two submitted well written essays.

____ 3. Omar after youre finished vacuuming will you please help me fold the laundry make the bed and take out the trash

____ 4. Please choose two of the following activities for winter carnival; ice skating, snow sculpture, sledding, ice hockey, cross-country skiing, and snowshoeing.

____ 5. Benjamin Franklin—a statesman, a scientist, an inventor, and a philosopher—was one of our Founding Fathers.

179

Punctuation Review II

Write a paragraph about what you think your life will be like in ten years. Do not include punctuation. Write sentences that should include commas, quotation marks, apostrophes, semicolons, colons, hyphens, dashes, and parentheses. Then exchange your paragraph with a classmate and fill in the punctuation. When finished, return paragraphs and check to see if your classmate correctly filled in all the missing punctuation.

Daily Warm-Ups: Grammar & Usage

180

1. Concrete nouns name people, places, and things. Abstract nouns name ideas. Lists of concrete and abstract nouns will vary.

2. 1. C; 2. C; 3. A; 4. A; 5. C; 6. A; 7. C; 8. A; 9. A; 10. C; 11. C; 12. A

3. 1. <u>grandmother</u>, **United States, Ireland, Great Depression;** 2. <u>brother</u>, <u>school</u>, **Toyota Camry;** 3. **Ryan,** <u>nights</u>, <u>weekends</u>, **Parker's Restaurant;** 4. **Aunt Hilda, iPod,** <u>birthday</u>; 5. <u>high school</u>, <u>college</u>, **Boston University**

4. Answers will vary.

5. Compound: first aid, home run, post office, washing machine, sleeping bag, paperback, fish tank, bystander, greenhouse, motorcycle, software Collective: gang, group, crew, league, crowd, tribe, family, orchestra, herd, committee

6. 1. Bianca and Erin went to the mall to shop for **their** prom dresses. 2. Jamie found the exact dress that **she** was looking for. 3. Erin found a dress that **she** loved, but **it** wasn't **her** size. 4. The salesperson helped Erin look for **her** dress in another color.

7.

First Person Singular/Plural	I, me, my, mine we, us, our, ours
Second Person Singular/Plural	you, your, yours you, your, yours
Third Person Singular/Plural	he, him, his, she, her, hers, it, its they, them, their, theirs

8. 1. **Mrs. Edwards,** <u>her</u>; 2. **Jorge, Derek,** <u>they</u>; 3. **gym,** <u>it</u>; 4. **mother,** <u>her</u>, **children,** <u>they</u>, <u>their</u>; 5. **Miranda,** <u>her</u>, **test,** <u>she</u>, <u>it</u>

9. 1. herself, R; 2. yourself, I; 3. himself, R; 4. herself, I; 5. myself, R

10. Lists will vary but may include all, another, any, anybody, anyone, anything, both, each, either, everybody, everyone, everything, few, many, most, neither, nobody, none, no one, nothing, others,

several, some, someone. Sentences will vary.

11. 1. <u>Who</u>, **that**; 2. <u>Whose</u>, **this**; 3. **these**; 4. <u>Which</u>, **that**; 5. **those**; 6. <u>What</u>

12. 1. reflexive or intensive; 2. interrogative; 3. indefinite; 4. demonstrative; 5. personal; 6. indefinite; 7. personal; 8. demonstrative; 9. interrogative; 10. indefinite; 11. personal; 12. intensive

13. 1. raised, asked; 2. popped; 3. flew; 4. applied; 5. rode; 6. ate, watched

14. 1. A; 2. A; 3. B; 4. A; 5. B

15. 1. T; 2. I; 3. T; 4. T; 5. I; 6. I

16. Answers will vary but should include many of the following: is, am, are, was, were, be, being, been, has, have, had, do, does, did, may, might, must, can, could, shall, should, will, would

17. 1. will be finished; 2. should write; 3. are giving; 4. is going; 5. might take; 6. have been running; 7. was rushing; 8. were looking

18. 1. Y; 2. N; 3. Y; 4. Y; 5. N

19. Paragraphs will vary.

20. Sentences will vary.

21. Answers will vary.

22. Sentences will vary.

23. Adjectives will vary.

24. 1. <u>well-dressed</u>, **French**; 2. <u>fifteen-minute</u>, **American**; 3. <u>three-headed</u>; 4. **Boston**; 5. <u>fair-skinned</u>, high-heeled

25. 1. a; 2. an; 3. an; 4. a; 5. a; 6. an; 7. a; 8. a; 9. an; 10. a; 11. an; 12. a

26. 1. favorite, the, tall, black; 2. a, long, exhausting, the; 3. The, excessive; 4. a, gorgeous; 5. a, stunning, gold; 6. The, narrow; 7. two, delicious, the, Italian; 8. The, little, a , pink, new

27. Sentences will vary.

28. The following should be checked: 2, 3, 5, 6, 8, 9, 11, 13, 14, 15

29. 1. carefully; 2. basically; 3. easily; 4. comfortably; 5. rarely; 6. happily; 7. drastically; 8. quickly; 9. equally; 10. variably; 11. barely; 12. terribly

30. 1. already, too, quickly; 2. quietly, outside; 3. sometimes, usually; 4. ever, again; 5. Yesterday, today; 6. eagerly, near; 7. more, later; 8. rather, well

31. Sentences will vary.

32. 1. <u>a</u>, <u>fluffy white</u>, <u>the</u>; 2. **patiently**, <u>a snow</u>; 3. <u>the</u>, <u>a</u>, <u>an</u>, <u>extra</u>, <u>ten-minute</u>; 4. **eagerly**, <u>warm</u>, <u>cozy</u>; 5. **Fortunately**, <u>three</u>, **too**, <u>late</u>, <u>previous</u>

33. 1. onto; 2. to, with; 3. until; 4. during; 5. beside, at; 6. no preposition

34. Lists will vary but may include the following: about, above, across, after, against, along, among, around, at, before, behind, below, beneath, beside, between, beyond, by, down, during, for, from, in, inside, into, of, off, on, onto, out, outside, over, through, throughout, to, toward, under, up, upon, with, within, without

35. 1. either, or; 2. whether, or; 3. but; 4. and; 5. not only, but also; 6. and

36. Sentences will vary. Suggested answers: 1. I remembered my book, but I forgot my homework. 2. I got home from school early, so I watched television for an hour. 3. I want to visit the art museum, or I want to visit the museum of natural history. 4. I fell skiing down the mountain, and I broke my wrist. 5. I got eleven hours of sleep last night, yet I still feel tired.

37. Sentences will vary.

38. Examples will vary.

39. 1. a word that names a person, place, thing, or idea; 2. a word that takes the place of one or more nouns; used to eliminate repetition; 3. a word that expresses action or being; 4. a word that describes a noun or a pronoun; 5. a word that modifies a verb, adjective, or other adverb; 6. a word that shows the relationship between a noun or pronoun and another word in the sentence; 7. a word that joins other words or groups of words; 8. a word or group of words that shows feeling

40. Answers will vary.

Daily Warm-Ups: Grammar & Usage

41. 1. S; 2. S; 3. F; 4. S; 5. S; 6. F
42. Sentences will vary.
43. 1. interrogative; 2. imperative; 3. exclamatory; 4. declarative; 5. interrogative; 6. imperative; 7. declarative; 8. exclamatory
44. 1. puppy, played; 2. Henry, bought; 3. Kaylee, locked; 4. Kyle, took
45. 1. A **slice** of apple pie; 2. The little black **dog**; 3. The **lady** across the street; 4. My **sister** Tiana; 5. **Anthony**
46. 1. **chased** our car down the street; 2. **baked** us cookies when we moved in; 3. **knows** how to make jewelry; 4. always **gives** tests on Mondays Sentences will vary.
47. Sentences will vary.
48. 1. Y; 2. N; 3. Y; 4. Y; 5. N; 6. N
49. Sentences will vary.
50. 1. me; 2. you; 3. class; 4. me; 5. you; 6. Ella
51. 1. sent (V), e-mail (D), Mr. Hernandez (I); 2. gave (V), gift certificate (D), grandmother (I);

3. mailed (V), bill (D), parents (I); 4. made (V), card (D), father (I); 5. read (V), story (D), kindergartners (I); 6. threw (V), fastball (D), batter (I)
52. 1. dancer (PN), Emily (S); 2. pets (PN), dogs (S); 3. instructor (PN), Mr. Lopez (S); 4. player (PN), Sanjay (S); 5. asset (PN), John (S)
53. 1. N; 2. Y; 3. Y; 4. Y; 5. N; 6. N
54. Sentences will vary.
55. 1. shy (PA), teacher (S); 2. beautiful (PA), flowers (S); 3. hot (PA), it (S); 4. old and tired (PA), dog (S); 5. smart (PA), teacher (S)
56. 1. RA; 2. PA; 3. PA; 4. RA; 5. PA; 6. RA
57. 1. PN; 2. PA; 3. PA; 4. PA; 5. PN; 6. PN; 7. PN; 8. PA
58. 1. contains two or more subjects, uses the same verb, and is joined by a conjunction such as *and* or *or*; 2. contains two or more verbs, uses the same subject, and is joined by a conjunction such as *and* or *or*; 3. a noun or pronoun that receives the

action of the verb; 4. part of a sentence that follows an action verb and comes between the verb and the direct object; 5. a noun or pronoun that completes the linking verb; 6. an adjective that follows a linking verb and describes the subject

59. Sentences will vary.
60. Paragraphs will vary.
61. Sentences will vary.
62. 1. **girl** <u>on the bus</u>; 2. **students** <u>in the auditorium</u>; 3. **homework** <u>for that class</u>; 4. **shade** <u>of pink</u>; 5. **baby** <u>across the hall</u>
63. 1. **angry** <u>with me</u>; 2. **crossed,** <u>with great satisfaction</u>; 3. **slept** <u>during our flight</u>; 4. <u>Because of our hunger</u>, **ordered**; 5. **pass,** <u>with your help</u>
64. 1. where; 2. how; 3. when; 4. why; 5. how; 6. where
65. 1. ADJ; 2. ADV; 3. ADV; 4. ADJ; 5. ADV; 6. ADJ
66. 1. Tyrone (A); 2. a book by Sylvia Plath (AP); 3. the capital city of Massachusetts (AP); 4. my

favorite instrument (AP); 5. Mr. Manchester (A)
67. Sentences will vary.
68. Sentences will vary.
69. Sentences may vary slightly. 1. We had my favorite, brownie sundaes, for dessert. 2. Sophie, my cousin, plays the violin well. 3. I read a great book, *The Joy Luck Club*, last week. 4. Have you seen my parents' friend Pedro? 5. The Morins, our neighbors, are moving next week. 6. Britney, a skier, pulled a ligament in a race.
70. 1. burnt; 2. screeching; 3. howling, camping; 4. torn
71. Participles will vary.
72. 1. <u>Driving to school</u>, **Raymond;** 2. <u>Reviewing her notes</u>, **Jackie;** 3. **test,** <u>printed on both sides of the paper;</u> 4. <u>Tired from his long day</u>, **Kasim;** 5. **Mrs. Goodman,** <u>walking up and down the aisles</u>
73. 1. <u>Landing safely on the runway</u>, the plane neared the airport. 2. The children, <u>covered in mud</u>, ran through the kitchen. 3. The vegetables <u>grown in</u>

<u>my garden</u> are organic. 4. The students <u>talking during the movie</u> had to stay after class.

74. All sentences should be checked except for number 1. Sentences will vary.
75. 1. Hiking up the mountain; 2. doing my homework; 3. raking the lawn; 4. Flying over the Grand Canyon; 5. smoking cigarettes; 6. Pushing this button
76. Sentences will vary.
77. 1. G; 2. P; 3. P; 4. G; 5. G; 6. P
78. Answers will vary.
79. 1. to speak clearly; 2. to send flowers to the neighbors; 3. To pass the test; 4. to try surfing; 5. To avoid getting in trouble; 6. to change my mind
80. 1. G; 2. I; 3. P; 4. P; 5. G; 6. P; 7. I; 8. I
81. 1. C; 2. P; 3. P; 4. C; 5. P; 6. P; 7. C; 8. C
82. Answers will vary slightly. 1. I am going to bed, and you should, too. 2. Grant's birthday is in April, and Selim's is in May. 3. I have Mr. Lopez for English, and my sister has Mrs. Thomas. 4. My favorite class is biology, and Shannon's is geometry.
83. Sentences will vary.
84. 1. S; 2. I; 3. S; 4. I; 5. I; 6. S
85. 1. whenever your mother gets home; 2. if it rains tomorrow; 3. so I wouldn't forget it; 4. after it had started; 5. while I make the salad; 6. before they burn
86. Sentences will vary.
87. Sentences will vary.
88. 1. which is downstairs on the coffee table; 2. that has a headlight out; 3. who got in the car accident; 4. that we take every day; 5. who wrote this paper; 6. who takes a hands-on approach; 7. that I just bought; 8. who gave that assignment
89. 1. **that** <u>you bought last week</u>; 2. **when** <u>we went shopping</u>; 3. **where** <u>we stayed</u>; 4. **that** <u>Isabel attends</u>; 5. **who** <u>passed the test</u>; 6. **which** <u>was left over from dinner</u>

90. Answers will vary slightly. 1. The waiter, whose name escapes me, brought us our breakfast. 2. The store where I bought my jeans is in the mall. 3. My mother rented me a movie, which is about airplanes. 4. The restaurant where the customers got food poisoning was shut down. 5. My sister goes everywhere in her car, which she bought herself.

91. 1. Our neighbor, who makes a great apple pie, is Mrs. Kimball. 2. no commas necessary; 3. That book, which is the best book I have ever read, is over there. 4. no commas necessary; 5. no commas necessary

92. 1. How much I weigh; 2. whoever writes the best essay; 3. what I can handle right now; 4. where diamonds are found; 5. how he did the trick

93. Sentences will vary.

94. 1. ADJ; 2. N; 3. ADV; 4. ADV; 5. ADJ; 6. N; 7. ADJ; 8. ADV

95. Sentences will vary.

96. 1. S; 2. C; 3. S; 4. C; 5. S; 6. C

97. 1. C; 2. CC: 3. CC; 4. C

98. 1. I forgot your birthday because I didn't write it on my calendar. 2. Here is my history paper that you wanted to read before I handed it in. 3. Grandma brought strawberry pie, which was a big hit. 4. Since it is raining, we are going to the movies instead. 5. Where is Monica? She was supposed to help me study.

99. Answers may vary slightly. 1. I broke my leg, so the doctor took an X ray. 2. Kyle got a new laptop, and he uses it all the time. 3. Thanh went to bed early because he wasn't feeling well. 4. Angela wrote a short story. She won an award for it. 5. Samantha got her license. She practiced for hours the day before her test.

100. Sentences will vary.

101. Principal parts and sentences will vary.

102. Regular verbs and charts will vary.

103. Principal parts and sentences will vary.

104. Irregular verbs and charts will vary. Irregular verbs may include buy, catch, feel, find, get, keep, lead, lose, say, seek, send, sit, teach, think, and tell.

105. Irregular verbs, principal parts, and sentences will vary.

106. 1. grown; 2. threw; 3. known; 4. took; 5. give

107. 1. beginning, began, begun; 2. drinking, drank, drunk; 3. shrinking, shrank, shrunk; 4. singing, sang, sung; 5. sinking, sank, sunk; 6. swimming, swam, swum

108. 1. gone; 2. fell; 3. ridden; 4. ate; 5. wore; 6. run; 7. came; 8. written

109. 1. brought; 2. making; 3. sold; 4. spoken; 5. stole; 6. draw; 7. known; 8. saw

110. 1. I; 2. I; 3. C; 4. I; 5. C; 6. I; 7. C; 8. I

111. 1. C; 2. I; 3. C; 4. I; 5. C

112. 1. sit; 2. setting; 3. sitting; 4. sitting; 5. sat; 6. sets

113. Sentences will vary.

114. call; called; will call; have called; had called; will have called

115. cook; cooked; will cook; have cooked; had cooked; will have cooked. Sentences will vary.

116. Chart 1: drive; driving; drove; have driven
Chart 2: drive; drove; will drive; have driven; had driven; will have driven

117. 1. Past tense verbs are formed by adding *-ed* or *-d* to the present form, unless it's an irregular verb. 2. Future tense is formed by adding *will* or *shall* to the present form. 3. Present perfect tense is formed by adding *has* or *have* to the past form. 4. The past perfect tense is formed by adding *had* to the past form. 5. Future perfect tense is formed by adding *will have* or *shall have* to the past form.

118. 1. future perfect; 2. present perfect; 3. future; 4. present perfect; 5. past perfect; 6. present

119. Sentences will vary. Verb forms: am traveling; was traveling; will be traveling; have been traveling; had been traveling; will have been traveling

120. Sentences will vary.

121. 1. P; 2. A; 3. A; 4. P; 5. P; 6 A

122. 1. were making; 2. has; 3. are; 4. plays
123. The following sentences should be checked: 2, 4, 7
124. Sentences will vary.
125. Sentences will vary.
126. Objective singular: me, you, him, her, it. Objective plural: us, you, them. Possessive singular: my, mine, your, yours, his, her, hers, its. Possessive plural: our, ours, your, yours, their, theirs.
127. 1. I; 2. We; 3. she; 4. she; 5. He; 6. I; 7. I; 8. they
128. The following should be checked: 2, 5, 8
129. Sentences will vary.
130. 1. who; 2. whom; 3. who; 4. whom; 5. whom; 6. who; 7. who; 8. whom
131. The following should be checked: 2, 4, 6
132. Sentences will vary.
133. The following sentences should be checked: 1, 2, 5. Sentences will vary.
134. Paragraphs will vary.
135. Answers will vary.
136. 1. younger, youngest; 2. brighter, brightest; 3. quieter, quietest; 4. nicer, nicest
137. 1. more interesting, most interesting; 2. smaller, smallest; 3. more delicious, most delicious; 4. funnier, funniest; 5. friendlier, friendliest; 6. more careful, most careful
138. 1. worse, worst; 2. better, best; 3. more, most; 4. less, least; 5. more, most
139. 1. most delicious; 2. better; 3. more beautiful; 4. friendliest; 5. taller; 6. tougher
140. Sentences will vary.
141. Advertisements will vary.
142. 1. well; 2. good; 3. well; 4. well; 5. good; 6. well, good
143. Sentences will vary.
144. The following sentences are suggestions for those that should have been rewritten: 1. You don't need any shoes. 2. We never catch anything when we go fishing. 4. We didn't have any of the new uniforms for our game.

145. 1. quick; 2. loudly; 3. slowly; 4. eager; 5. nervously; 6. proud
146. E-mails will vary.
147. 1. My, Amy, I; 2. My, Bentley; 3. Ashok, Mom's, Kenny; 4. Should, I, Russells; 5. Irina, I, Elizabeth's; Sentences will vary.
148. Geographical names will vary.
149. 1. Have, Mount Rushmore; 2. Mount Rushmore, Black Hills, South Dakota; 3. We, summer; 4. We, Midwest; 5. We, Garcias; 6. Their; 7. On, Mississippi River; 8. Next, Grand Canyon
150. Examples will vary.
151. Paragraphs will vary.
152. The following should be checked: 2, 3, 5, 7, 8, 9
153. 1. My, mother, French, Canadian; 2. We, Italian; 3. Our, German, Hans; 4. The, Irish, Hans; 5. Carlos, Swiss, Europe; 6. Alaskan, seafood, market; 7. I, American, Indian; 8. You, British
154. 1. Have, Coach, Hancock; 2. It, Grandma; 3. My; 4. The, senator; 5. Auntie; 6. I, father
155. Answers will vary.
156. 1. Someday, I, Washington; 2. My, dad, street, Volkswagen, Jetta; 3. On, September, I; 4. My, Mrs. Kennedy, She, English; 5. On, California, San Diego; 6. Our, Wallingford Way; 7. This, summer, I, Boston Red Sox, Park; 8. My, grandmother, Irish, grandfather, Italian
157. 1. the Civil War; 2. my dad; 3. Labor Day in September; 4. Lake Erie; 5. the governor of Indiana; 6. the *Boston Globe*; 7. my brother Martin; 8. correct; 9. Algebra I and Geometry; 10. summer in Maine; 11. the Democratic Party; 12. correct
158. Sentences will vary.
159. The following sentences should be checked: 2, 5, 7, 9
160. Rules for capitalization include the following: first word in a sentence, first word in a line of poetry, the pronoun I, salutations and closings in letters and e-mails, names of people and animals,

geographical names (towns/cities, streets, counties, states, countries, regions, continents, islands, mountains, bodies of water, stars, planets), names of groups (organizations, businesses, institutions, government agencies, political parties, teams), time periods and events (days, months, holidays, historical events, historical periods, special events), documents, nationalities, races, religions, languages, awards, brand names, bridges, buildings, memorials, monuments, vehicles, academic courses, technological terms, proper adjectives, titles of people, titles showing family relationships, and titles of written works, plays, television programs, movies, and works of art.

161. 1. IN, question mark; 2. ES, two exclamation points; 3. DS, period; 4. IM, period or exclamation point; 5. IM, period or exclamation point

162. Abbreviations and sentences will vary. *Bonus:* State abbreviations do not contain periods.

163. 1. I will attend Boston College, the University of Massachusetts, or Harvard. 2. My mother, my father, and my sister all went to Boston College. 3. My friends are attending colleges in California, Colorado, and Florida. 4. What college I attend depends on what I get for financial aid, what scholarships I am awarded, and how much money my parents can contribute. 5. I am excited about college, but first I have to be accepted, complete my senior project, and graduate from high school.

164. 1. N; 2. C; 3. C; 4. N

165. Answers will vary. Sample answers: 1. My favorite fruit is watermelon, but my sister's is kiwi. 2. I am on the baseball team, and Kendra is on the track team. 3. Billy rode his bike, and his mother walked the dog. 4. Tawana put up the tent, and Jacob built a fire.

166. 1. If you want to go to the concert, you have to get tickets immediately. 2. In 2001, terrorists flew planes into the World Trade Center. 3. Listening to the lecture, I realized I left my notes at home.

4. Under several stacks of paper, I found my application. 5. Since you weren't here yesterday, we decided to do the presentation without you.

167.   E-mails will vary.

168.   1. The teachers, I believe, are all in a meeting. 2. Where, Mr. Beckett, do you suggest I write my reply? 3. To tell you the truth, Leah, I've never heard of anything like that. 4. This car, on the other hand, seems as though it will suit your needs. 5. Kristy, please hand me the remote. 6. I do, however, think I can finish my essay by tomorrow.

169.   The following sentences should be checked: 2, 3, 5, 8

170.   Paragraphs will vary.

171.   Answers will vary but may include the following: items in a series, adjectives before a noun, compound sentences, introductory elements, dates and addresses, salutations and closings of letters/e-mails, addressing a person directly, parenthetical expressions, appositives, and nonessential participle phrases and clauses.

172.   1. We have to recite Frost's "Stopping by Woods on a Snowy Evening." 2. When I was younger, my favorite book was *Tuck Everlasting*. 3. I love almost all Disney movies, but my favorite is *The Little Mermaid*. 4. That was a wonderful rendition of "America the Beautiful." 5. My father reads the *Wall Street Journal* every morning. 6. One of my favorite episodes of *Friends* was "The One Where Everybody Finds Out."

173.   1. "Hannah, have you read Maya Angelou's poem 'Phenomenal Woman'?" Mr. Harrison asked. 2. no quotation marks needed 3. "That building over there," he said, "is the tallest building in the city." 4. Did you hear your grandmother say "happy birthday"? 5. I think the chapter titled "The Ghost Returns" is the scariest part of the novel. 6. no quotation marks needed

174.   1. Simon's; 2. women's; 3. everyone's; 4. players';

5. Travis's; 6. sister-in-law's 7. can't; 8. he's; 9. they're; 10. you'd; Sentences will vary.

175. 1. C; 2. I; 3. I; 4. C; 5. C; 6. I

176. Sentences will vary.

177. Sentences will vary.

178. 1. Where is the girl—she just moved in across the street—going? 2. We walked (or should I say crawled) back to our hotel room after a long day. 3. Three teachers—Mr. Dugan, Ms. Ortiz, and Ms. Thayer—are all nominated for the Teacher of the Year award. 4. That puppy (often found sleeping in his cage) bites my fingers when he plays. Sentences will vary.

179. 1. C 2. I; Out of all twenty-one of you, only two submitted well-written essays. 3. I; Omar, after you're finished vacuuming, will you please help me fold the laundry, make the bed, and take out the trash? 4. I; Please choose two of the following activities for winter carnival: ice skating, snow sculpture, sledding, ice hockey, cross-country skiing, and snow shoeing. 5. C

180. Paragraphs will vary.

Turn downtime into learning time!

For information on other titles in the

Daily Warm-Ups series,

visit our web site: walch.com